transformational
TEACHING

IN THE INFORMATION AGE

SUSTAINABLE
FORESTRY
INITIATIVE

Certified Fiber Sourcing

www.sfiprogram.org

THOMAS R. **ROSEBROUGH** | RALPH G. **LEVERETT**

transformational

TEACHING

IN THE INFORMATION AGE

MAKING WHY AND HOW WE TEACH
RELEVANT TO STUDENTS

Alexandria, Virginia USA

1703 N. Beauregard St. • Alexandria, VA 22311-1714 USA
Phone: 800-933-2723 or 703-578-9600 • Fax: 703-575-5400
Web site: www.ascd.org • E-mail: member@ascd.org
Author guidelines: www.ascd.org/write

Gene R. Carter, *Executive Director;* Judy Zimny, *Chief Program Development Officer,* Nancy Modrak, *Publisher;* Scott Willis, *Director, Book Acquisitions & Development;* Carolyn Pool, *Acquisitions Editor;* Julie Houtz, *Director, Book Editing & Production;* Darcie Russell, *Editor;* Reece Quiñones, *Senior Graphic Designer;* Mike Kalyan, *Production Manager;* Cynthia Stock, *Typesetter*

All web links in this book are correct as of the publication date below but may have become inactive or otherwise modified since that time. If you notice a deactivated or changed link, please e-mail books@ascd.org with the words "Link Update" in the subject line. In your message, please specify the web link, the book title, and the page number on which the link appears.

PAPERBACK ISBN: 978-1-4166-1090-8   ASCD product #110078   n1/11
Also available as an e-book (see Books in Print for the ISBNs)

Quantity discounts for the paperback edition only: 10–49 copies, 10%; 50+ copies, 15%; for 1,000 or more copies, call 800-933-2723, ext. 5634, or 703-575-5634. For desk copies: member@ascd.org.

Library of Congress Cataloging-in-Publication Data

Rosebrough, Thomas R.
  Transformational teaching in the information age : making why and how we teach relevant to students / Thomas R. Rosebrough and Ralph G. Leverett.
    p.   cm.
  Includes bibliographical references and index.
  ISBN 978-1-4166-1090-8 (pbk. : alk. paper)
  1. Effective teaching. I. Leverett, Ralph Geist. II. Title.
  LB1025.3.R67 2011
  371.102—dc22
                              2010035632

20 19 18 17 16 15 14 13 12 11   1 2 3 4 5 6 7 8 9 10 11 12

To Elsy and John, my faithful parents, who gave me opportunities they never had; and to Edith Ross, who has blessed my life with her loving spirit. To Dr. Alexander Frazier for his inspiration. To Bonnie, whose love sustains me. And, to hope for the future for Andi and Elijah.

—Tom

To my daughter, Heather, who has taught me transformational teaching; to Houston, a middle school student whose skills demonstrate fully the transformed student; and to Karl and Mildred Kratz, who transformed me.

—Ralph

transformational
TEACHING
IN THE INFORMATION AGE

MAKING WHY AND HOW WE TEACH
RELEVANT TO STUDENTS

PREFACE

I n education it seems too easy to lose our way, to forget where we
have been and who we are. Poet W. H. Auden says that human
beings are distinctive from animals in at least three ways: We
work; we laugh; and we pray. The best teachers are the most human
teachers, but the modern era can conspire to deny our best qualities. We live in an age where more people can access information
faster and in more diverse forms than ever before. This wondrous
reality has magnified a problem. We are in danger of consuming
huge amounts of information divorced from purpose and meaning.
"Why" and "because" are often casualties in the quest for an education to match the perception and challenges of this time. *Transformational Teaching in the Information Age: Making Why and How We
Teach Relevant to Students* is an integrative project that seeks to reaf-
firm the identity of education by exploring pedagogy from a timeless perspective that places learners in the center of the classroom
and asks why we teach those learners. It offers the notion that as
teachers we have not taught until our students have learned. And it
describes our mission in education as being transformational rather
than informational.

The Transformational Pedagogy Model is the basis for and thread throughout this book. The model seeks to offer a creative perspective through all its extensions, from synthesizing seminal and contemporary knowledge in the fields of pedagogy and educational philosophy, to adding psychological and neurobiological information as applied to teaching and learning. This is a practitioner's text because it applies learning theory to pedagogy. It moves the teacher from pedagogical concepts to an understanding of how to teach to transform and illuminate. This book is also for the teacher who likes to reflect upon the challenge of connecting the two great goals in education: academic and social.

For almost 30 years we have taught public school students, state university students, and Christian university students. All students are the inspiration for this writing. We are indebted to them: elementary, middle, and high school students, undergraduate and graduate learners whose wonderful curiosity and dedication formed the focus for the book. As a reflection of our educational discourse with them, some of their stories appear in this book, but the names of the students and most of the teachers are intentionally fictitious. We are grateful for our students and colleagues at Union University who encouraged us and who helped us field-test this writing through the lenses of their experience. They all have had stories to tell, and we are better for their experiences.

We also wish to acknowledge the graphic support of Todd Mullins and Sarah Belcher as well as the administrative support of Helen Fowler and Christy Wyatt. Our gratitude also goes to contributors Jane Anderson Scholl, Ann Singleton, Tom Stanton, and Teresa Collard for their "teaching stories," as well as to Ron Hosse for his editorial analysis. A very special thanks is reserved for our editors at ASCD, Carolyn Pool and Darcie Russell, for their patient and insightful guidance.

Our deepest expression of gratitude is owed to our families. Bonnie, Tom's wife, is the love and friend of his life and has patiently and prayerfully encouraged him in everything, including this writing. And Chris and Tim, Tom's sons, have illuminated his life. Heather, Ralph's daughter, has long been a source of inspiration and encouragement to him.

We offer this book to the everlasting vision of nurturing the individual potential of students.

INTRODUCTION

To say we live in a fast-paced and changing era is an understatement. The rate at which knowledge is exploding and the ease at which information is accessible are breathtaking. In 1969 the late Neil Postman and Charles Weingartner wrote about change in *Teaching as a Subversive Activity* using a clock tuned to the rate of communications inventions. They employed the clock as a metaphor of 3,000 years (1 minute = 50 years) to demonstrate how in the past two centuries (last 4 minutes) so much has happened so fast: 11 minutes ago the printing press; 4 minutes ago the locomotive and telegraph; within the last 3 minutes the telephone, photograph, radio, automobile, motion pictures, and airplanes. Television appeared less than 2 minutes ago. Lasers, communications satellites, and computers were invented in the last minute. Within the last 30 seconds, the Internet and the personal computer appear. Within the last 5 seconds have come cell phones, digital technology, biotechnology, smart phones, and more. Before 11 minutes ago on this clock, we would have to return to the invention of writing itself, close to the beginning of recorded time.

Postman and Weingartner asserted that their clock would show the same pattern with other invention-concepts like medicine or science: 2 minutes ago, antibiotics; 1 minute ago, open heart surgery; 1 second ago, statin drugs. The sheer volume of information and knowledge is increasing at an unprecedented pace. Their concept was that change has changed. The degree of change is new.

Although it is easy to exaggerate change and become fixated on our own age as though this world has never experienced change before, their point seems valid. As they add, "Just when we have identified a workable system (of values, beliefs, and patterns of behavior), it turns out to be irrelevant because so much has changed while we were doing it" (p. 11). Change happens whether we name it or not, and behavior patterns can die slowly.

Many teachers still believe they are in the information-giving business, which was perhaps reasonable until a minute or two ago on Postman and Weingartner's clock. In a poignant film from a few years ago, *Finding Neverland,* Mrs. Snow asks *Peter Pan* author James Barrie, "I suppose it is all the work of the ticking crocodile, isn't it? Time is chasing after all of us, isn't that right?" Our point: Time chases information as well as people.

Many teachers have the tendency to put their heads down, noses on grindstone, and plow straight ahead through what it is they think they are supposed to be teaching. Suddenly they look up to see that not only has the subject matter changed almost overnight, but that students themselves have changed. All this of course is symptomatic of Alvin Toffler's future shock, where we are confronted by the notion that the world we were educated to believe in does not exist. What we are teaching today may be obsolete in the immediate future.

Thomas Friedman (2007) argues persuasively that we are living in a unique period and that our world is flat. Indeed, transportation and communication advances in the past few centuries have reduced the world's size from medium to small. Since 2000 many technological factors came together, creating a newfound power for individuals to collaborate and compete globally through a "flat-world platform" (p. 10). A flat world, in which everyone and everything is easily accessible to everyone else, is made possible in part by the convergence of the personal computer, fiber-optic cable, and the rise of workflow software.

Friedman says change is so different now because individuals are being empowered "to plug in and play" to connect globally. Most tellingly, to ensure their job survival, these individuals must focus on "value-added" or risk having their work outsourced. What is your value-added as a teacher? What is the difference *you* make? How educators perceive this value-added for our learners is crucial and is a theme of this book. How can teachers cope with such a new world? We think a beginning point is to understand why we are teaching in the first place.

Informational Teaching

The Information Age centers upon computer technology and the converting, storing, retrieving, and transmitting of information. Wikipedia (2008), itself a controversial creation of the digital age, defines the Information Age as being a global economy shift in focus from producing goods (the Industrial Age) to manipulating information. Indeed, even the process of finding this wiki-definition is a testament to the digital age. We were part of over 2.7 billion searches on Google during a single month in 2008 (Fisch, 2008). As we write this book, the offer has come for training on Web 2.0 online tools called Zotero, Ning, Podomatic, Technorati, and PB Wiki. We would compare the initially bewildering verbiage to mass transit, with disembodied-sounding intercom announcements of street stops. It is a new day. There are strong implications for educators' adjustment to this new age, especially for why and how we teach.

Efforts in schools to teach standards-based curricula in lock-step fashion, to evaluate learning through standardized examination, and to punish educators for quantifiable failings on test score gains are all symptoms of how the Information Age is changing educational systems. One important coping mechanism that can be used to make sense of these advances as they relate to education is to ask key questions. Through it all, we must stay focused on foundational questions that go beyond "What do we teach?" and "How do we assess it?" to

"What does it all mean?" "What should schools be doing?" "What is the teacher's role?" "Who are we teaching?" "How do learners learn?" and "How should we teach?" Ultimately, the question is "Why do we teach?" Unless we are careful and mindful, education's mission is lost.

We can all agree upon some purposes for education, including fostering a lifelong learning ethic, teaching for deep understanding, and developing students who care not only about achievement but about other people. Brooks (2004) says that the "issue at hand isn't our lack of collective knowledge or ability. It's our lack of collective vision and will. We don't do a very good job of creating the classrooms we want" (p. 9). We agree with this assessment and would add that educational goals must be reprioritized.

Jackie, a teacher, said that she longs for schooling to be first about the students as persons and then about results. One unsettling characteristic of education in the Information Age is the demand for uniformity and conformity. Education standards in many states call for programmed "sameness." For example, all 5th grade teachers in some districts must teach the same skill from the same text using lessons from the same website on the same day. Urban districts are particularly obsessed with standardization because many of their schools have been placed on a failing schools list. Standards have made many teachers feel they are not trusted; they feel commanded into an oppression of teaching to dogmatic policies. Uniformity and conformity march together.

Add to this schema the alliance of political and business "essentialist" leadership, and we have "informational teaching" as a dominating pedagogy in education. It is pedagogy with little concern for deep understanding and even less concern for the values of socialization. The thinking in classrooms has generally gone like this: We have subject matter to cover, not enough time to do it well, and the test is looming and daunting because successful schooling now seems to be mostly about raising achievement scores. When others suggest different priorities like teaching the whole child, they are accused, as Marge Scherer (2007) relates, of being "squishy and subjective" (p. 7).

As teachers we may want to linger, enjoy some discussion, ask some more questions, allow students to think, talk, and ask questions, spend some time outside class in dialogue, express some interest in their lives. Time is our enemy, however, and we must move on. Concern with a deeply intellectually satisfying and socially responsible life is important, but not what teachers are paid to do. Current priorities in schooling have consequences.

Fully two out of every five teachers (40 percent) in the United States are disheartened about or disappointed with their jobs (Yarrow, 2009), according to a research study funded by the Gates and Joyce foundations and conducted after the 2009 school year. Attitudes and motivations of teachers are vital, and critical as to why they entered teaching as a profession. Most teachers will say, if we ask them, that they chose to be a teacher because they want to profoundly affect the lives of their students. No doubt, teachers *live* for moments like the joy of hearing a 1st grader read fluently or seeing a shy child begin to exhibit leadership qualities. As a teacher, excitement and fulfillment come from watching a student learn. When students learn and change, teachers change, too. However, teachers now find that the focus is on academic knowledge or on the essentials of this kind of knowledge. The job, the mission, is to spur measurable achievement in our students, and there the priority is found.

Why not such a priority as achievement? A generation of students, especially disadvantaged youth, has not only fallen behind but lost its way. The solution, however, is a single-minded focus on essential skills and accountability. In public schools this priority is a reality. No Child Left Behind has been an obvious culprit, although some would say NCLB was a reflection of misguided thinking that has been evident in schooling for many years. Focusing on the intellect alone denies children's complete identities. A fulfilled life requires more than intellectual pursuits.

Help Wanted: Nurturing Teachers

Nurturing teachers are needed. Our early 21st century students have grown up with an access to information through technology that is mind-numbing. They often demonstrate only a veneer of learning. They have been convinced that their disaggregated information is knowledge, and they place great confidence in their presumed under-standing. Our students seem busier than before, but their lives are hardly turned toward academic pursuits. Instead of these pursuits, we find a different kind of immersion. Our students are attendants in the kingdom of electronic devices where learning is more finger based than brain based. A recent software management commercial is close to the point when it asks, "Is the question 'How can I get more information?' or is it 'How can I put it all together?'"

Nurturing is needed at many levels to build the kind of deep understanding that transforms individuals. Great teachers not only call students to new levels of inquiry that build deep learning, but also model a social and spiritual authority that is missing in our students' lives. Robin Collins (2009) relates how she began knitting together her 5th graders at Columbine Elementary School in Wood-land Park, Colorado:

> To heighten awareness of interdependence, I tried a new group-building activity. At one weekly meeting, as each student complimented someone, he or she tossed a ball of yarn to another student in the circle, first wrap-ping the yarn around a hand or finger. We continued to toss the ball back and forth until we built a web. Once we were entangled, I elicited students' observations. (p. 82)

Students' observations deepened to the point that they realized the web shook when someone moved "because we are all connected." As educators we can find ourselves far from this vision of connectedness, instead disfigured by the isolating forces of an otherwise wondrous time in history. Myopia is a symptom of such isolation. Educational myopia occurs when we cannot seem to see what is directly in front of us: our students! We do not see our students when we fail to see who they really are and when we fail to teach to how they learn.

For example, most teachers' dispositions seem to lie more natu-rally with analysis than synthesis. Indeed, many of us may have cho-sen the profession of teaching because of our ability to break down a concept or idea or piece of knowledge so that it is more understand-able for our learners—an important teaching skill. We think that if we can just show our learners how simple a concept is, they will get it. So we begin with small details. The big picture of teaching and learning involves synthesis, however, and can only be clearly focused when all aspects are considered and taken as a whole. It may seem counterintuitive, but the great majority of learners understand new concepts when the subject is introduced generally before it is described or taught specifically (Bransford, Brown, & Cocking, 2000; Sawyer, 2006). Yet we often teach inductively, the opposite way from how most of our students learn.

Carlos discovered how his students learn best when he was crafting a bulletin board for his classroom. He was only able to finish about half of the project before his 8th grade students came to class. They were so intrigued by the question, "What makes people people?" that they harassed him most of the day to finish the bulletin board. Carlos suddenly realized that it would be best if his students helped finish the project. So, he made it a learning tool as he went about meeting his original objectives.

The bulletin board was completed by the students as an inquiry lesson with sociological, anthropological, biological, and historical implications. Carlos was so impressed by his students' response to his "discovery" that he made the pedagogy of inquiry an integral part of his teaching repertoire. The desire to complete the incomplete seems built into most learners, which is one way of thinking about deductive learning. Carlos mindfully honored the way his students learned.

What Matters?

It is easy for teachers to become confused about what really matters in the classroom. The grand scheme of U.S. education in the 21st century, indeed globally, would seem to deny a more holistic perspective on what we might generally refer to as "respect for the learner." Results-oriented education is in vogue with test scores serving as not only evidence of learning but learning itself.

While this achievement paradigm certainly has merit and validity—graduates must compete in the global marketplace—it is part of a bigger picture of focusing on the goals of education. While objective measurements are an important part of schooling and one indicator of success, it is important not to overreach. Every child or adolescent is more than a future employee. And, each of us is far more complex than our scores on standardized tests. What really matters in education is not what but who.

Robert Sternberg (2008) calls for us to assess what matters: learners without expiration dates. He asserts that we need schools that teach to the analytical, to the creative, to the practical, and to wisdom, which surely represents a moral dimension of education. His notion is that we should teach students to become active and engaged citizens of the world. In contrast, "if we teach only for facts, rather than for how to go beyond facts, we teach students how to get out of date" (p. 21). Teachers ultimately respect our students when we believe that they are more than vessels for knowledge. We can teach for holism *and* depth.

The values of life, of citizenship, and of being a moral person are social goals that must be placed beside the 3 R's and in lieu of the 4 T's (teaching to the test). It is an issue of academic integrity that our focus must be allowed to shift to our students. Priorities and attitudes make a difference. We desire, and our students deserve, nothing less than the transformation of our students in mind, body, and spirit.

Organization of the Book

Attitudinal openness to richer dimensions of knowledge demands that we listen to ourselves and to others, but it also requires that we ask foundational questions and formulate principles that define our concept. The book is organized into two sections. Part 1 is the educational philosophy section where basic assumptions and beliefs about teaching are addressed, such as Why do we teach? What is our fundamental motivation for teaching? What goals are important? Why do teachers teach to some goals but exclude others? Who are we as teachers and learners? What fundamental roles do teachers play in the classroom? What does it mean to teach the whole student? Why should teachers place students at the heart of their teaching?

Part 2 is the educational psychology and pedagogy section where classroom process and behavioral concepts are explored and we examine ideas and questions, including What is teaching as compared to learning? How do students learn? Why is process so important in teaching and learning? How can teachers teach students how to learn? Why are questions so vital to teaching and learning? How do we teach by asking questions? How can teachers engage learners?

Part 1 asks many *Why* questions because philosophy and theory demand a variety of arguments, theories, and justifications of our points of view. Formulating a response to *why* or accepting anyone's response to the question is also theological because the response requires something of an abiding faith and trust in authority. We recognize that asking why necessitates asking who teaches and who learns. Leaving it there is not sufficient for educators. Part 2 asks many *How* questions and is necessary architecturally in psychology and pedagogy, because teachers must be responsible for planning what can happen after explaining their rationale for education, for supporting the rationale with evidence, and for moving from theory to practice. Thus, we will conceptually begin with *why* and move into *how* later in the book.

With the two parts of the book, we formulate eight principles of transformational teaching, with one chapter for each principle:

Part 1. Why We Teach: Relevant Concepts
    1. Inspire Your Students
    2. Embrace Your Role as a Whole Teacher
    3. Teach the Whole Student
    4. Place Students in the Center
Part 2. How We Teach: Relevant Strategies
    5. Teach for Learning
    6. Know How Students Learn
    7. Teach Students How to Learn
    8. Teach by Asking Questions

In addition to the organization of the chapters, we have included special ideas that we would like you to "take away" with you when you finish reading the book. These ideas are prefaced with an arrow and are meant to provide further explanation of and insight into the text (see p. 17). The goal is to provide clarity, application, and understanding throughout the book.

part
ONE

The little town that time forgot,
that the decades cannot improve.

Garrison Keillor

1

INSPIRE YOUR STUDENTS

Great men are they that see that spiritual is stronger than any material force, that thoughts rule the world.

Ralph Waldo Emerson

Why do we teach? Certainly we teach to inform, but we must also teach to inspire. Most of us want to change a learner's life for the better. Finding confidence through the study of a subject makes a life better. Doing well on an exam is an important part of life. Learners are more than a sponge for academic content, and they are more than a test score. Holism in our goal setting is vital, and thinking collectively is helpful in the complex profession we call teaching. Complex is the descriptor because people are complex and, hence, learning itself is complex. If learning were as simple as adding to a knowledge storehouse in the brain, we could just sit our students in front of computers 100 percent of the time and dismiss all teachers.

Our rapidly changing global culture makes the search for pedagogical authority more elusive than ever. U.S. education, which is historically and politically embedded in our ideal of a better life, is fragmented as never before. The conjunction *or* holds sway in our thinking, as when we think we must stop enriching teaching as we teach basic skills, or as we focus only on achievement to the demise of considering students' unique aspirations. But we do not have to choose between *who* we teach and *what* we teach. We can do both even as we prioritize the *who* in education: our students.

We propose a return to schooling where education begins with learners and their *transformation,* where the teacher-student dynamic is spotlighted, where the academic and the social are meant to be connected and combined, and where the social is once again joined with spiritual meaning and transcendence.

Judy was working with her 6th grade students on "The Baboon's Umbrella," a fable from Arnold Lobel's 1980 classic children's book, *Fables.* Simple, but laden with profound meaning, this story is about Baboon holding open an umbrella on a sunny day, complaining that his umbrella is stuck. His friend, Gibbon, advises him to cut some holes in the umbrella so that the sun will shine through. After Baboon does so, rain begins to pour, soaking him to the skin. Lobel's moral (p. 12) is "Advice from friends is like the weather. Some of it good; some of it bad."

When Judy asked her learners what they thought of the story, Anika raised her hand and said, "My moral would be 'Do your own thinking.'" Judy asked her to elaborate, and she said, "It is silly to let your friends think for you. We might as well be baboons to do that, even though some of my friends have some good ideas." The story inspired Anika to think through an important concept, one with dimensions deeper and broader than the intellect.

Inspiring students does not require stories with morals, but we think it requires teachers who can think beyond single goal structures. Transformational teaching goes beyond the academic into the other great goal of education: socialization. In the realm of socialization goals, however, the meaning of social has splintered, separating it unintentionally or deliberately from spiritual illumination. We assert that the dynamic found between teachers and learners can have a sacred quality, and that these human relationships depend upon connections that are indeed spiritual in essence.

Students need teachers they can believe in: teachers who model lives of empathy and service. Social and spiritual goals should be aimed toward the same end: serving something or someone greater than ourselves. Emerson said that "our chief want is someone who will inspire us to be what we could be." Being what we can be reflects the potential of the human spirit. To capture the emotions and ignite the interest of learners has not only academic but social and spiritual contexts.

The Transformational Pedagogy Model

If we believe that teaching is a mere imparting of information, we have surely aimed too low. To hit the bull's-eye, we need to aim above the target of academic achievement. Learners need teachers who will, as Aristotle remarked, show them the *good*. The Greek educator used the term *arête* to describe virtue modeled by a good person. *Arête* represents a combination of skill, wisdom, power, and passion for good (Willard, 1998). Teachers need to be encouraged and affirmed in their roles, in their potential for transforming lives, and in their calling to the real needs of learners. That learners *need* teachers to guide them in their learning is a cognitive principle with affective underpinnings.

Expert teachers know the structure of their academic discipline, and novice learners need their guidance in grasping it. But learners also need the authority of sensitive mentoring as they struggle with overcoming conceptual barriers within the discipline and within their own experiences. "Who has influenced your life the most?" is an important question for both students and teachers. How students feel in a classroom may be, in the long view, more important than what they know. By envisioning pedagogy as meeting the needs of the whole person, by perceiving education as both heart and science, and by believing that teaching is about helping students find self-fulfillment through enriching knowledge, the holism and depth of learning can be embraced.

The Transformational Pedagogy Model is designed to demonstrate that holism in education can have a transformational quality. Figure 1.1 illustrates the relationship between the learner and three categories of educational goals. We define transformational pedagogy as an act of teaching designed to change the learner academically, socially, and spiritually. Transformational teaching begins with the learner, and transformational learning involves deep understanding and occurs in classrooms where teachers have high expectations. The principle is that raising student achievement is the floor, not the ceiling. Higher achievement is a by-product of teaching to a holism of goals and to a depth of understanding. We can reach the whole child through inspiration and a more reflective perception of our role as educators.

FIGURE 1.1
Transformational Pedagogy Model

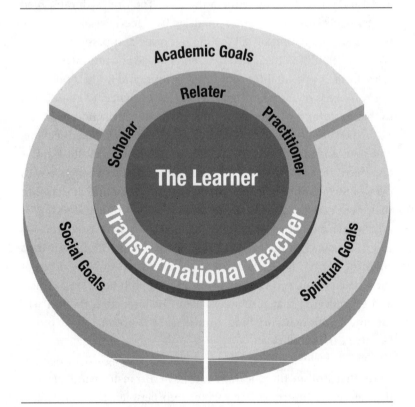

We must look for transformational opportunities. Teachers know, for example, that assessment is not an isolated entity but is a part of the fabric of instruction. Teachers evaluate their students both formatively and summatively, but most learning takes place formatively (i.e., along the way). Students need teachers who communicate that they believe in students and all their potential. Overemphasis on summative assessment can discourage learners, but, in fact, any assessment that is less than sensitive to learning needs is misplaced in schools. For example, Rick Stiggins (2007) argues that the assessment process can lend itself to reclaiming student-centered instruction: "Even the most valid and reliable assessment cannot be regarded as high quality if it causes a student to give up" (p. 25). Transformational teaching includes a concern for a person's ultimate welfare and potential, for teaching students as well as subjects. This means that the way teachers think and learners *feel* in school transcends the curriculum. Students' feelings are a response to what the school or the teacher has done to satisfy or fulfill their needs as unique individuals.

 The Power of Touch

Marian Diamond and her associates, pioneers in brain research, tell an interesting story based on "rat experiments" they were doing along with some counterparts in Japan. They noticed that in the two controlled environments geographically separated, with all other variables held constant, the "Japanese rats" lived longer than the "American rats." After further careful differentiation, they discovered a saliently important difference between the two environments. When American rats had their cages cleaned, they were allowed to simply climb into another cage. When the rats in Japan were given clean cages, they were briefly held by the research assistants before transfer. The human touch created a longer life span! Students need the therapeutic power of a transformational teacher who "touches" and transforms lives.

Teachers' feelings are vital, too, because they sustain teachers' dedication to their calling and affect those involved directly and indirectly in schools. The calling to be a teacher involves placing the whole learner at the center of teaching. Schools are only as effective as their teachers, the best of whom require and inspire many dimensions of support. As many experienced teachers know, students and teachers should expect education to be a mutually transforming experience. To teach is to be changed, as much as or even more than the learner is changed. To transform is to effect change. *Transform* is an "action" word. The goal is to make teaching a "trans-action," to conceive of teaching as an action across the teacher-learner gap. And, within this transaction, a transformation can take place. How can teachers teach in the holistic way demanded by the Transformational Pedagogy Model?

Using a holistic approach to teaching does not require a formula learned in teacher education courses. Instead, holistic education comes from a relationship built by sensitive teachers using pedagogy attuned to the academic, social, and spiritual needs of learners. In 2009, Roslyn taught a lesson focused on a celebration of the anniversary of Abraham Lincoln's 200th birthday. Mandy, an 11th grade African American student, asked what the Emancipation Proclamation really meant: "Did it mean freedom for black people in America?" Roslyn answered the question with a question: "Mandy, what does freedom mean to you?" Her student's answer was "It means having choices and opportunities like everyone else." To which Roslyn said, "I think the answer to your question is that it was a beginning of a difficult process, but it was a new beginning." Then, Roslyn asked, "Has there ever been a time when you felt like you were given a new beginning?" This question inspired a deep discussion in the class, centered not just on the intellectual understandings from Lincoln's crisis leadership but also on deeper, even spiritual implications for students' lives. This teacher's evaluative questions are holistic pedagogy attuned to deep understanding of students' needs.

 ### Emotions Affect Learning

Why are student and teacher feelings important for educational success? Neurobiological studies are confirming what teachers have known for a long time: *We remember what we feel.* Where were you September 11, 2001? Where were you when Barack

Obama was inaugurated? What do you remember about the day? Chances are that certain memories are vivid. Learning and memory formation are prompted by episodes, places, and our emotional reactions. Emotion often motivates us to learn all we can about a topic, prompting an insatiable curiosity to explore all the issues and events that follow an important situation in our lives. We learn best through this "episodic memory" because our total being is challenged and engaged. We are holistic learners.

....

Pedagogy is the art and science of instruction; the term is derived from the Roman term *pedagogues*, educated Greek slaves who escorted Roman children to school. Pedagogy, in a strict sense, relates to how we teach. Pedagogy involves many sensitive decisions, such as when and how to apply understanding of many different teaching strategies to various educational situations. Implicit in this decision-making process is the concept of responsibility for our choices, especially those that affect others. Moral concern for the learner is implicit in the calling of teaching.

Moral concern for our students begins with building respectful relationships. As Ruby Payne (2008) has found, the verbal and non-verbal signals a teacher transmits are a vital part of showing respect for students. Interactions between teachers and students living in poverty, for example, can include greeting them with "Hi" and calling students by name, smiling, using eye contact, answering questions, talking respectfully instead of judgmentally, and helping those who need help. Everyday behaviors communicate simple respect. Establishing mutual respect can be transformational.

Transformational pedagogy integrates teaching the whole learner, rather than attending separately to academic, social, and spiritual goals. These three goals are united, even synergistic, when we pay close attention to whom we teach and why we teach. A more holistic ethic seeks to understand education in all its complexity and in all its dimensions. Miller (1997) says that holistic education is "based on the premise that each person finds identity, meaning and purpose in life through connections to the community, to the natural world, and to spiritual values such as compassion and peace" (p. 1). How can teachers transform learners academically, socially, and spiritually? Being mindful of and wise about education's purposes is a beginning.

Reflecting on Purpose

Self-fulfillment is a liberating part of education, perhaps the most important purpose of education. As teachers we want our students to be successful, but we must be careful not to narrow the meaning of the concept. Pedagogy can make the difference in education, especially if pedagogy is guided by not just the questions "How?" and "What?" but also the questions "Why?" and "Who?" Teaching can be linked to domains of knowledge *and* the science of learning, and teaching can be viewed as holistic. The message is that we as teachers can attain these lofty goals if we have the will to seek them.

Nathaniel is a middle-grade student who just knew he could not read. After years of failure, he had stored up enough emotional roadblocks to give up the effort. Then he met his 6th grade teacher, Iretta. She pulled him aside, looked him in the eyes, and promised him that this year would change his life. Together they would succeed. She knew Nathaniel had the desire to be a reader, even though he acted otherwise. Iretta built on that desire, helping him succeed little by little, working together until he could read independently. It was not so much what she did that made the difference; it was *who* she was in the relationship with the learner. Iretta's belief in Nathaniel changed his life.

It seems likely that the reader will notice the spiritual goal category of the Transformational Pedagogy Model first. We recognize the risk in including it in the model. For some who read this book, it is an automatic road block. For many educators it may conjure images of soft education, yet another form of coddling students. For others it may engender distrust for hidden agendas of religious dogma and public school lawsuits. Laura Rendon (2009) reflects on the spiritual concept as being potentially divisive: "Some individuals may be pro-religion and antispirituality. Some may consider themselves spiritual but not religious. Others view spirituality in conflict with Judeo-Christian values" (p. 27). Divisive or not, we think people are spiritual beings in their essence. The simplest acts of teaching and the well-chosen words of a teacher, such as those spoken by Iretta, constitute spiritual action. She saw Nathaniel's frustration from repeated failure, helped him persist until he succeeded in reading, and helped him transform his life.

A concern for issues that affect the human spirit is an integral part of a teacher's calling. Teachers with courage to believe they can connect to the transcendent can realize goals beyond the academic and even the social. Teachers who contribute to encouraging students to desire lives of fulfillment meet a most worthy teaching goal. Why should we consider spiritual goals as an integral part of teaching and learning? The simple answer is the relationship formed between Iretta and Nathaniel. Motivation and hope are part of the spiritual goal dimension.

Without the spiritual component, human beings are machine-like with a wondrous compilation of bones, organs, and senses (Sire, 2004). The rationalist chooses to reject the spiritual altogether. Though we know spiritual transformation as a goal and a process will not be accepted universally, we believe it is a crucial element forming the foundation of transformational pedagogy.

For our purposes we choose simplicity: Transformation is an illuminating change in head and heart that helps learners achieve their potential and their purpose. *Head* refers to our human capacity to discover and problem-solve. *Heart* is an ancient concept used synonymously with a person's essence or soul. Head and heart work together to animate who we are. Who we are is what poet Stanley Kunitz calls our "indestructible essence" (Braham, 2006). Teachers are called to activate the spiritual essence in every learner.

The Teacher-Student Dynamic

Many of us believe that schools exist to transform individuals by teaching societal knowledge and values *and* to transform society by being an institution for social reform. That's the larger context of schooling. In this book, we focus more on the personal, teacher-student dynamic. We believe that the Information Age exacerbates human tendencies to prioritize the larger education goals, and to minimize, and thus deprioritize, attention to the importance of the individual teacher and learner. Educators and policymakers tend to spend a lot of time at the system or policy level and forget about individual students and the creative abilities of those who teach them. Knowledge in the informational culture that our students inhabit is changing quickly, making it more important for teachers to connect curriculum to their learners' lives.

One example of the tendency to focus on the larger context of educational goals (Hood, 2009) is the trend to departmentalize instruction at younger levels. Some schools, in their desire to use subject specialists, are requiring 6-year-old elementary students to change classrooms and teachers during the school day. Having more than one teacher for young children is not necessarily a bad thing. From our holistic perspective, this early departmentalization trend prioritizes school systems' efforts to raise test scores over the more commanding priority of the sociospiritual well-being of children. Schools have no solid evidence that specialists improve young children's achievement scores, yet much like ability-grouping practices of old, we jump to conclusions based on thinking that having teachers focusing on fewer subjects is a logical way of meeting achievement test goals. We think, however, that schools and especially teachers must focus on holistic, family-style support systems as a priority. Transformational teaching places learners' total academic, social, and spiritual welfare at the center of our philosophy of teaching.

 Horizontal Versus Vertical Grouping

Horace Mann, the father of U.S. public education, adopted our school model from Prussia. The horizontal grouping of ages replaced the vertical grouping of the one-room schoolhouse. Teachers were to become grade specialists, with the reasoning that by placing like-age groups together, teachers could be much more efficient. Unfortunately, this efficiency sometimes fails us, like when we become convinced that everyone can be taught the same lesson if they are the same age. With every year the gaps grow wider in students' reading levels. Or, if we can just group people together with similar test scores (ability grouping), much more learning will ensue. No, scores do not significantly change for the better, and self-esteem issues abound. In contrast, vertical grouping (having students of different ages work together) promotes a differentiated pedagogy because it forces learners to engage. Transformational teachers need academic efficiency, but not at the expense of individual, personal engagement.

....

We ask for teachers to be "transformers." Transformational teaching is a higher standard for teachers, and it places more demands on learners' potential. Descriptions of teaching and learning usually focus on the learner as a biological entity. For example, Piaget (1926) realized early on that the social environment, which includes the role of language and education, as well as the physical environment were the sources of new knowledge. Such a model of learning serves us well if we limit ourselves to biological conceptions of the learner.

Transformation involves more than a biological understanding of learners. Dare we reach beyond the empirical world of observation and experimentation to a spiritual dimension in learning? Belief in the human spirit's potential can include the world of how teachers think about, perceive, and relate to their students; and illumination, whether intellectual or spiritual, can include how learners feel inside as a positive response to their teachers' belief in them. This transformation, while aimed at the learner, often includes mutually transforming relationships between teachers and learners.

Both concepts are what acclaimed environmental scientist John Houghton (2006) terms the "fifth dimension of the spiritual," beyond material length-width-depth, beyond Einstein's time dimension. This fifth dimension has an enormous effect on the other four, an idea sometimes lost in the Information Age. This extra dimension is one that educators know is there because it includes the world of thought, of knowing ourselves as thinking, conscious human beings. This human element beyond the material and temporal defines us—it is our human spirit. In education, the spiritual is the dimension of relationship between teacher and student, a zone of caring communicated by a transformational teacher. The foundation of this spiritual dimension consists of trust and respect. When students and teachers do not trust and respect each other, it is an issue of the human spirit, a dimension that affects schooling because it directly affects the teacher-learner relationship.

Anna, a 16-year-old, is experiencing some strong emotions. She learned recently that her parents were divorcing. Her teacher, William, knew something was wrong because her personality changed from sunny to very moody. He knew that adolescents, for example, react strongly to divorce and may reflect attitudes that are destructive to the learning process. No simple solutions are available with such complex human emotions, but William pledged to be patient and understanding and respectful of her new life. Every day he observed carefully and listened intently to Anna, empathizing but not patronizing her feelings. He did not pretend to know what she was going through. Instead he told her, "I understand you are hurting and I can support you." Every day he sought to build consistency into Anna's routines with as few surprises as possible. Sensitive and courageous teachers who try to understand and respect the experiences of these learners can affect the total growth of their students. For teachers as well as principals, heart is the issue. Joanne Rooney (2009) addresses the issue of the *essence* of our students from a principal's viewpoint:

> Principals talked about children in their schools, noting that their essence cannot be condensed into efficiently scored, disaggregated data. Data tools are useful. But even a dramatic increase in test scores headlined in the newspaper must not become the end product of our educational endeavors. What's going on in the hearts and minds of our students must always make the headlines of the teachers' attention. (p. 87)

Most of all, great teachers respect their learners by believing in the potential of their students. Consider the concern for children in America left behind by poverty and low achievement. Ladson-Billings (2006) argues that it is not what teachers do with disadvantaged students, but what they believe and how they think about them that make a difference in successful teaching. She writes about "culturally relevant teachers" who see learners as full of possibilities, who view students from a position of *informed empathy*, who "feel with the students rather than to feel for them. Feeling with the students builds a sense of solidarity between the teacher and students but does not excuse students from working hard in pursuit of excellence" (p. 31). Such a combination of support and challenge can bring academic, social, and spiritual illumination to students' lives. By illuminating change in the lives of students, those students' lives can be improved.

Illumination

In a film called *The Majestic,* Jim Carrey plays Luke, a young World War II veteran. The story centers on Lawson, California, a town that lost more than three dozen of its sons to war. Nearly a decade later the mourning townspeople were inspired by the return of Luke, formerly missing in action. The townspeople are inspired to help rebuild a beautiful old theater that was owned by Luke and his father. The theater is a wonderful metaphor. Before Luke's return, the cinema was dark and rundown. When the lever is pulled to relight the marquee, the darkness is illuminated with multicolor lights spelling T-H-E M-A-J-E-S-T-I-C in vertical cascades of color: The town was awakened from its grieving stupor.

Teachers and students in classrooms can pull levers of light. Rafe Esquith (2007), a 5th grade teacher in Los Angeles who teaches at a school where 92 percent of the children live below the poverty level, explains what happened as he earnestly tried to light his student's alcohol burner:

> For that one moment, the only thing that mattered to me was that this girl should have a successful experiment. She was going home that day with a smile on her face. I bent closely over the wick of her alcohol lamp. . . . I leaned as close as I could, and with a long kitchen match tried to reach it. . . . The wick caught fire, and I looked up triumphantly to see the smile I expected on the girl's face. Instead, she took one look at me and began screaming in fear. I did not understand why they were all pointing at me, until I realized that while I was lighting the lamp, the flame had touched my hair. (p. xi)

In trying to light the alcohol burner, Mr. Esquith set his hair on fire and didn't even know it until the kids started screaming. Later he commented that as ridiculous as that was, he actually thought, if he could care so much he didn't even know his hair was on fire, he was moving in the right direction as a teacher. Truly, an illuminating moment for teacher and students!

When we teach to a synergy of goals to the whole person, transformation includes illumination. How teachers view their students is a part of a belief system that affects learning. What we believe makes a difference not only in what we do but also in what we think we can do. Teaching is not only individual; it is personal. Spiritual illumination and academic understanding are within the grasp of the human mind; they are certainly not mutually exclusive, and they can be complementary.

 Different Kinds of Illumination

Illumination can be seen as spiritual, but it is also quite academic, temporal, and cognitive. We all know "classroom illumination" when the learner gains a moment of insight as a potential solution suddenly comes into awareness. But, even in schools with good reputations, we find "darkening" worksheets everywhere, ill-led group activities, mindless lessons, and drill-and-kill teaching to standards. There is something special about light: Artists live for it. Photographers study the slanting effects of early day or evening light to achieve the perfect picture. Painters who have mastered its effects are revered: Michelangelo, Rembrandt, da Vinci, Monet, and Van Gogh. Teachers who master the multiple dimensions of educational illumination change lives with their words and actions.

We readily accept that teachers can bring "light upon a subject" academically, but what about socially or spiritually? Illumination can have a spiritual meaning in a broader, humanistic sense. Jerome Bruner (1996) writes about having a "surer sense of what to teach to whom and how to go about teaching it in such a way that it will make those taught more effective, less alienated, and better human beings" (p. 118). To teach so that our students are able to know, are able to do, and are able to be better persons is a holistic notion borrowed from classical liberal arts education and lacking in many schools, colleges, and universities.

Illumination, as we have discussed, is multidimensional in intellectual and spiritual enlightenment. The Transformational Pedagogy Model includes these dimensions. Transformation as a goal stands in contrast to the more limited ends of the Information Age. Indeed, we are contrasting spiritual goals with the more concrete and temporary dimensions of academic or social goals, even as we allow the three goals to *synergize*, working together to create a deeper understanding of our world.

Spiritual goals are personal, timeless, subjective, and social, which is precisely why they are vital to learning. Human beings are personal, timeless, subjective, and social. We include the spiritual in holistic teaching, especially in the conception of the learner. Educators (Huebner, 1999) have taught the "whole child" for decades; surely this is one of the more metaphysical conceptions by educators or psychologists. As Perkins-Gough (2008) says it, we "again need to restore balance in education" (p. 96). It is vital that teaching be seen once again as a reaching beyond our more limited motivations to a spiritual summons. We must teach to inspire. Learners need the inspiration of teachers to find and reach their purpose in life.

Three Goals in Synergy

It is not sufficient to focus only on the spiritual because it truncates our comprehensive purposes as educators. The three distinct goals work in synergy in the model, and they are all integral parts of the two great goals of education: academic goals and social goals. Academic goals spring from the traditional liberal arts as well as professional education. Mastery of the constructs of the academic domains, with their attending depths of relevant information, is as vital as ever. As we discuss later in this book, guided inquiry teaching can help students plumb the riches of academic understanding.

The other traditional goal of schooling is social. Indeed, not so long ago, "social" was often found in a spiritual context of transcendently serving others. We were taught to be social not because of what it could do for us, but because of what it could do for others. We separate the "spiritual" from the social in the Transformational Pedagogy Model for emphasis. Social goals, as we describe them here, are designed to improve human welfare. They are relational, temporal, and self-directed. Teachers must plan for social goals like cooperation and responsibility. Cooperation in the classroom as an "enterprise in which all individuals have opportunity to contribute" and feel responsibility (Dewey, 1938, p. 56) is a classic social, even democratic, goal. Spiritual goals in the model deal with the dynamics of human relations and the human spirit, and include the transcendent values of hope and self-sacrifice.

Being open to new ideas and other perspectives is fundamental to liberal learning and to the personal illumination of learners, which can lead to their transformation. In the Information Age, holism and deep knowledge are needed in goal setting. A new transformational focus on "why we teach" and "who we teach" has implications for "how we teach."

Final Thoughts

In our rapidly changing world, many of us experience great angst that our schools and students are being left behind. It may seem counterintuitive, but we must slow down and realize that the present and future are connected to the past in some fundamental ways. Education seeks to bring relevance and meaning into the lives of students; therefore, the academic, social, and spiritual need not be disconnected. To succeed educationally we must first ask ourselves two basic questions: Why do we teach? Who are we teaching? Education is less about information and more about inspiration. The goals and purposes of pedagogy must be reconsidered. Education must be more than informational teaching, or the transfer of facts from the teacher to the learner. We must expect students to be equipped with skills *and* attitudes that will prepare them to face new challenges. This chapter introduced the Transformational Pedagogy Model, which prioritizes attention to the personal level and individuals in education, with a focus on the importance of the individual teacher and learner. The model extends the critical components of the social and spiritual, allowing for growth and understanding beyond facts and traditional applications. It is an education that cares about students and values their development. It goes beyond the obvious. It allows for holism and depth in these fractured times.

2

EMBRACE YOUR ROLE
AS A WHOLE TEACHER

The most common hope is that each class by its end will help them to become slightly different persons in some way. This hope transcends the subject matter of a class, or a student's background, or even whether the student is a wise old senior or an incoming freshman.

Richard Light

It takes a significant measure of hope to enter the teaching profession. It takes a whole teacher to teach a whole child. We teach to transform by being whole teachers. Earlier we introduced the contrast between informational teaching and transformational teaching. Informational teaching implies that the teacher holds all the knowledge and students are empty vessels to be filled. Transformational teaching implies that a fundamental change takes place among the members of a learning community. Let's explore in more detail what transformational teaching looks like in action. Then we will describe the roles played by a transformational teacher.

In education, hope is often substituted for self-efficacy, a belief within learners that they can be successful in specific ways. Hope is one life skill that occupies the spiritual dimension of education. It is an essential part of the mantra that *all* children can learn and succeed. Teaching with hope includes believing, really believing, in the potential of each and every learner, *and* communicating that belief to the learner. "Full of hope" is one descriptor for transformational teachers who are passionate and believe that the world of education is more than an information culture. Great teaching requires a total commitment to all the roles that affect learning. As teachers, we can all use reminders of those roles.

Sacred and Secular

An integral part of our transformational and holistic model is the presence of spiritual goals in the classroom. Although this idea may seem superfluous or even foreign to many who read this book, and skeptics may say, "Don't you know that our public schools are in an achievement crisis?" and "How can we even conceive of this notion in U.S. public schools?" we urge you to read on.

Our response is that the world of education and schooling and teaching is like every other human endeavor in at least one way. Every day, every week, every month, and every year we encounter our own crises of the spirit because we are human. Teaching, we contend, is like no other profession in its intensity, breadth, depth, and absolute importance. Why limit our teaching to the segmented world of test scores? Teaching effectively involves so much more than academic achievement. We should be asking instead why we would want to limit the education of our students.

To explore transformational teaching, we turn to a contrast that can readily address anyone concerned with teaching to the human spirit: the dynamic tension between the secular and the sacred in education. Barry Harvey (1999) drew an important conclusion while studying the Latin root, *saeculum,* of the word *secular.* Despite common conceptions of secular as worldly rather than spiritual, or evil rather than good, Harvey discovered that its meaning was not the opposite of sacred. Its root has more to do with the material versus the transcendent, or specifically, with time versus timeless.

Thus, secular thinking should not be seen as the opposite of sacred thinking. In fact, secular and sacred can be oddly complementary. We might think of the two concepts overlapping in a Venn diagram. It is an overlap of two rather different ways of seeing the world. Those who advocate sacred or spiritual goals are focusing on transcendent values, a sense of timelessness in an approach toward life. Secularists, by contrast, are very much grounded in this world with its space and time and matter. But what are we to make of the overlap itself? Why should we as teachers even care? Why should public schools be concerned about such a seemingly metaphysical concept?

The Venn overlap zone of sacred with secular might be thought of as our life's calling because it is where we find purpose, our passion to serve. In fact, we assert that the greatest transformational teachers overlap or integrate so strongly that the circles become one. Think about Socrates, Melanchthon, Comenius, Pestalozzi, Booker T. Washington, Mary Bethune, Montessori, and today's teachers including Jaime Escalante and Rafe Esquith. They were (or are) *in* the world but *overcame* their world; they all served higher purposes while toiling in secular societies with very real problems. We believe that the greatest teachers recognize that the sacred should not only overlap but actually integrate and illuminate the secular darkness.

Teachers are called to meet spiritual goals in the lives of their students. What does this mean? Surely a sense of the sacred includes concern for relationships between teachers and students as well as among teachers, schools, and parents. Richard Weissbourd (2009) writes that many schools have invested in character education programs designed to teach values including discipline, self-control, responsibility, and fairness. He also identifies another compelling fact: Despite their good intentions, schools have not been successful in positively affecting students' moral capacities with these programs. Weissbourd concludes that it is not teachers and schools who fail to teach values or social responsibility that changes lives in positive ways; rather, "it's the nature of the relationships that schools establish" (p. 28). The Transformational Pedagogy Model centers on the relationship among teachers and students. This pedagogical relationship affects learners academically, socially, and spiritually.

The teacher-student relationship can be an incubator for growing a sense of the sacred in secular lives. The Whole Child Initiative fostered by ASCD embraces the principle that teaching core subjects to meet academic goals is not enough for teaching students to achieve lifelong success. The initiative calls for five tenets in its approach to developing students who are healthy, safe, engaged, supported, and challenged. It is a holistic approach to teaching that embraces the academic while reaching beyond it to the needs of the whole learner.

For example, DiMartino and Clarke (2008) identify several problem areas for high schools that touch all five of the Whole Child tenets. Specifically, lack of adult support, invisibility, and isolation are three of their problem areas where high schools begin to fail their students. Lack of adult support is defined as students talking only to their peers because they do not see any alternatives. Invisibility means students feel invisible but crave recognition beyond their small group of friends. Finally, isolation occurs when teachers do not provide opportunities for their learners to engage the larger community beyond high school. Striving to meet the social, academic, emotional, and spiritual needs of learners would reach students in their very real worlds.

We experience the secular world every day, with its sights and sounds and human failings and successes. Perhaps teachers live in it like no other profession. Teachers are increasingly asked to change students' lives where other institutions like the family, the church, or the government have failed, abdicated, or misunderstood what learning is. Teachers who meet students at 8 a.m. on Monday see the angst and anxiety on students' faces, and they feel the pressure of improving test scores. But the best teachers still want desperately to teach the whole child. What attributes are needed for them to do this?

Know Yourself

Transformational teachers know themselves. They have considered their strengths and personal attributes. They have reflected upon what matters most to them. They have also analyzed whether their teaching reflects their core values. For example, if patience and compassion are core beliefs of teachers, do they practice equity for all students, even the ones who test them the most? Transformational teachers reflect on their daily interactions with students, making adjustments to maintain healthy relationships with learners.

Gwendolyn was the youngest of three daughters, and she was considered the least capable. Her teachers had unofficially labeled her as having severe intellectual disabilities. When Gwen reached the 6th grade, her new teacher refused to see limitations. Cheryl began exposing Gwen to a thematic curriculum that emphasized visual and tactile-kinesthetic learning styles.

By the end of the school year, Gwen was demonstrating 87 percent mastery of the total curriculum. As this example demonstrates, the concept of equity does not mean equal treatment; it means accommodating and challenging students according to their needs. Gwen's academic progress was suffering, and Cheryl used patience and compassion to help Gwen overcome a stigma. In this complementary way, timeless values affect our secular realities.

Making the effort to be holistic in education is important. Focusing solely on the academic excludes social or spiritual goals, which by extension precludes a student-centered paradigm in favor of a subject-centered philosophy. New teachers cutting their teeth on an accountability climate seem more likely to accept this reality of essentialism as not only acceptable but sufficient. B. F. Skinner would say they have been "conditioned" in the learning of their craft. The academics of teaching foundational skills in reading and mathematics overtake their initial, idealistic desire to teach the whole child.

It is common to hear new teachers, as well as experienced teachers, identifying themselves by citing their record on raised achievement scores. We become the proverbial frogs boiled in gradually heated water: Instead of jumping out and teaching to transform the whole learner, we find ourselves conforming to an educational culture that should be unacceptable.

 ## Quality, Not Quantity

Some educators have concluded that the more direct content teaching time they spend, the more their students will learn. Jackson (2009) calls for change in this kind of thinking and believes that teachers need to prioritize their time by quality not quantity, observing that master teachers "spend more time planning than teaching, and asking students questions rather than talking themselves" (p. 156).

Mindful teaching with the goal of making a difference in students' lives is the thesis of this book. Teaching for transformation involves not only a holistic perspective for the teacher but also a deep understanding for the learner. Let's describe the attributes of a transformational teacher.

The Transformational Teacher

Jaclyn teaches a kindergarten class of 26 children, including Amanda, a 5-year-old who is quite challenging. Actually, Amanda is not a child emotionally because she is the oldest of 6 children with a 21-year-old mother. Jaclyn knew that she had to confront a problem: Amanda sought to control the other children as well as her teacher by using the iron resolve she had learned at home. One day Jaclyn took the children for a long walk outside on the school property and made a point to walk with Amanda. By simply walking and talking together and using what Ladson-Billings (2006, p. 31) calls "informed empathy," Jaclyn was able to forge a new relationship built upon respect.

 Informed Empathy in Action

Empathy involves adopting another person's mind-set, which for an adult working with a child can be difficult. Occupying the intellectual or emotional landscape of a child or adolescent seems at best unlikely and at worst impossible. But, for teachers who pledge to listen with sensitivity and with cultural understanding, the task seems not so large. When empathy is informed, the teacher uses an understanding that is based on knowledge of human development and on knowledge of the student's culture. It is a caring that is disciplined toward high expectations.

In the Transformational Pedagogy Model we teach to transform, and learners are the focused target for transformation. If teachers allow themselves to be co-learners with their students, they are also changed by the teacher-student relationship. To effect change, academic, social, and spiritual goals must be in synergistic play. Since learners are at the center of our attention, their attributes and needs are worthy of reflection, study, and discussion (see Chapter 3). But the teachers who are the change agents also need to be analyzed and described. What attributes are possessed by transformational teachers? Describing them requires a discussion of the purposes of teaching.

Why Do We Teach?

Reaching learners requires mindful goal setting. Maintaining the distinction between what we teach and how we teach is important, even as we recognize the symbiotic link between knowledge and pedagogy. It seems, however, that we need a third conceptual member to form a teaching trilogy that focuses more on who we teach. Therefore, who we teach = why we teach!

Anthony teaches high school mathematics in a suburban setting on the West Coast of the United States. To him, teaching has always been about the subject, hierarchy, concepts, and algorithms of mathematics. He majored in math in college with a secondary education minor. At some level Anthony knows about human development and cultural understanding because he took those courses. He believes, however, that success in the content area for his students will take care of any "nurturing issues" learners might have. Besides, as he says, "Nurturing kids is for elementary teachers." So, his focus is achievement. What can be wrong with this approach?

We think Anthony may be short-sighted in his approach at best and tragically insensitive at worst. Transformational teachers are whole teachers because they use academic, social, and spiritual means to teach the whole child. We propose a new role construct for transformational teachers to help balance the demands of informational versus transformational teaching. This role construct, conceptualized in Figure 2.1, has three facets: scholar, practitioner, and relater. Educators who have reason to be superbly confident in their subject are called *scholars*. Teachers who specialize in methodology that engages learners are called pedagogues, or in more contemporary language, *practitioners*. What do we call teachers who have an abidingly deep

FIGURE 2.1
The Transformational Teacher

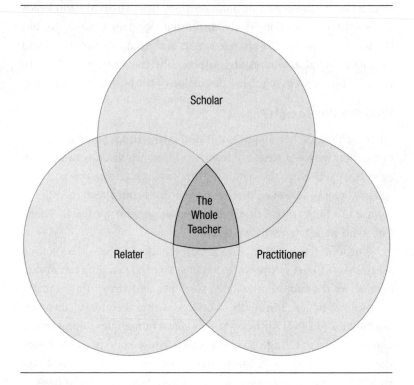

understanding of and concern for whom they are teaching? It seems there are many adjectives, like *sensitive, nurturing, empathetic,* or even *culturally competent.* We propose a noun, *relaters,* to describe teachers who nurture the pedagogic relationship, who care about and attend to their learners' essential natures as persons, their human potential.

Great teaching has always looked like this. The triad of roles played by the transformational teacher is to be enjoined to the whole learner. The small area of overlap is where we find the transformational teacher. It is significant that the area is small because it is quite uncommon that we find holistic teachers who fulfill the roles of scholar, practitioner, and relater. Each role can complement the others, but sadly for students, teachers often play only one or two roles as they teach.

Teacher-Scholars

Consider the scholar. It seems more vital than ever, to say it bluntly, that teachers know something. Some teachers are so disengaged from scholarship or burnt out from the academic life that they vow never to read any book other than perhaps some mindless fiction on a beach. These teachers fail in the worst way to model lifelong learning for their students. Every parent, teacher, and student knows a teacher who does just enough to get by in the content area. Such a teacher is education's bane.

The stereotyped version of a scholar is an unfortunate one, which is that those who teach must also be widely published. Most teachers just do not have the time it takes to write extensively, but they can make time to read and reflect. Many teachers contribute articles to newsletters and other periodicals, including online blogs. Others agree to speaking assignments locally, regionally, and nationally.

To achieve superb confidence in one's subject requires hard work. The human mind is amenable to reinvention and reinvigoration, but dedication to, and even love for, the task of learning is vital. The best teachers, the saying goes, are also the best learners. Scholars are curious about and embrace the world of ideas—they are in love with their subject or discipline. Enthusiasm for one's subject usually comes from knowing the subject at deeper and wider levels of understanding. This enthusiasm communicates socially and spiritually to learners.

Unfortunately, we all know teachers who seem to know their subject superbly but cannot teach it. This kind of teacher thinks that teaching is the same as presenting or lecturing, and never quite understands why her students don't "get it." Too often, however, teachers practice their craft on autopilot, relying upon their pedagogy to carry the day. Teachers may find themselves in a reactive mode because their students often reflect societal angst. Without seeking to be patronizing, U.S. public educators are part of a culture oppressed, woefully underappreciated, expected to absorb not only children's decreasing attention spans but also parents' and society's failure to model moral discipline.

On the other hand, teachers and schools can also disengage themselves from society instead of confronting the issues and seeking to engage their students. Reaction trumps pro-action for too many teachers. Scholarship begins to seem less important than finding "methods" to survive the day. After all, an achievement exam looms near. The practitioner role comes to the fore.

Teacher-Practitioners

Teachers who engage their students, who expertly practice the art and science of teaching on a daily basis, who routinely explore a variety of methodologies in their classrooms, are practitioners. Teacher-practitioners are doers who are always thinking of new ways to connect content to learners. Their students are engaged by their teacher's methods. The best practitioners offer not the standard three-course meal but a virtual smorgasbord of approaches to their subject area.

Teacher-practitioners at their best know their subject and know how their students learn. P–12 teachers who have made it their calling to be knowers (scholars) as well as doers in their classrooms ought to be recognized as scholar-practitioners. Pedagogy flows from scholarship in the content area as well as in human learning and development. Creative teachers are not produced in a vacuum, which is why both preservice and in-service teacher education focus on content knowledge, educational psychology, and pedagogy. Knowing who it is we are teaching and how we can connect to them is a complex mix, requiring knowledge as well as experience.

Scholarship and pedagogy must go together, and it surely cuts both ways. That is, good pedagogy withers apart from solid scholarship—teachers have to know something. In the end, it is the subject matter that engages the learner. The teacher is the transforming vehicle to carry the content to the student. Teachers who find their purpose in transforming learners know their subject and find joy in teaching students through a variety of strategies. The ultimate pedagogical prize in the classroom is student engagement.

→ Know Thyself

Teaching is as individual as learning, and it is important that we recognize this fact. Parker Palmer (1998) reminds us that "we teach who we are" (p. 2), but strong identity can easily turn to smug complacency. What do you consider strongest for you, knowledge of your subject or your creativity in methodology? Of course the response doesn't have to be one or the other, but most of us have to identify a weakness and work to improve. Perhaps the most important concept in teaching is Socrates' enduring counsel of "Know thyself."

It is a generalization with some accuracy that elementary teachers identify more strongly with the practitioner role, while secondary teachers resonate more with the scholar role. If teachers in P–12 seek to achieve proper esteem in the United States, they must model both of these roles at both levels. Modeling scholarship and pedagogy is not sufficient; informational teachers do that. Transformational teachers embody a third characteristic: They care about how they relate to their individual students.

Teacher-Relaters

We use the term *relaters* because we wish to emphasize the pedagogical relationship between teachers and students. Relaters meet social goals and spiritual goals in teaching. They have larger purposes in their teaching roles because they are committed to listening and responding to students' true identities. Teachers who relate are practicing a form of compassion, which is love in action. And, teacher-relaters are sensitive to the curriculum and how it is meeting academic, social, and spiritual goals.

This sensitivity is especially needed among teachers of adolescents. As Thomas Armstrong (2007) reminds us, the developmental growth of early adolescence allows for a new gain of metacognitive capacity. This capacity allows for not only academic growth but also engagement in and exploration of the real world outside the classroom. Schooling is not a race to the top; it is a journey for learners. With the assistance of teachers and schools, students can develop independence as they prepare for life beyond the classroom.

Elementary age students need relaters for different reasons. In early childhood education, the holistic capacity of play seems to have been forgotten by our schools and replaced by a focus on academic achievement. Children are unable to learn formal reading and mathematics operations until they are cognitively ready. This usually occurs at 6 or 7 years old. Pushing these skills on young children can result in emotional and cognitive blocks for failing students. Wise teachers who provide a multisensory and caring environment, what Friedrich Froebel termed a "garden for children," can stimulate emergent literacy as well as mathematical conceptual understanding.

Unfortunately, this third role of relater is one that many teachers either are not interested in or do not care enough to take the time to develop (or both). Focusing on the teacher-student relationship in the classroom is often blocked by a fear of stirring up conflict that may lie beneath the surface of students' thoughts and feelings. Students who need a nurturing teacher are most often the ones who are best at hiding it. It is the same with parents (Weissbourd, 2009), particularly low-income parents who are often suspicious of schools and teachers and may lack the advocacy skills needed to be effective communicators.

Also suppressing the relater role is time pressure. Many teachers, as we have said, are so overextended and so used to meeting more "objective" priorities that they convince themselves that the subjectivity of strengthening relationships is not their job. It is especially inconvenient to attend to weaknesses we have as teachers.

 Multiple Intelligences for Teachers

Howard Gardner says we all have multiple intelligences (strengths) that seem to come naturally and weaknesses that we must identify and enhance. For teachers, surely interpersonal (people skills) and intrapersonal intelligences (introspective skills) are essential for pedagogical success, but it's difficult to find both highly developed intelligences within the same person or teacher. Can we develop intelligences that we are lacking? Can we change the behavior or attitude in ourselves? It seems our only barrier is the human will.

The role of relater itself, however, has its challenges and challengers. Many state departments of education publish annual report cards for schools and school districts, labeling schools as succeeding or failing. Indeed, when we scan the grades given in subject areas for local schools, why should we care if an individual teacher relates to a student in failing school? At the federal level, one popular reform idea would tie teacher pay to student test scores. States are almost certain to connect to this idea because federal money is at stake. As long as test scores rise, no one rushes to question the more human issues in education. So, what could be wrong with this kind of achievement?

The construct is a macro-level one, much like an annual business or stockholders report. Investors judge the health of their company by its numbers. Such a business construct does not translate well to the full education of our children. Of course, there are concepts that our school leaders can learn from successful CEOs, like visionary planning and ethical mission statements. For example, some of the most enduring companies have made it their business to care first for the overall service to their customers, and then believe and expect that stockholders will benefit as a by-product. A profit-and-loss mentality, however, or any kind of closed commitment to an ideological educational system of doctrine, does not bode well for the overall academic, social, and spiritual well-being of students. Openness to ideas and best practices for enriching the human potential of our students is needed. Openness can be found in the human heart.

The Heart of Teaching

Heart is what teacher-relaters have and is the real but often hidden issue in contemporary discussions of how poverty affects students and schooling. A teacher-relater embodies compassion, courage, and the resolution to not give up on students. The academic goal structure in U.S. schools has achieved such primacy that socialization goals have suffered. Worse, spiritual goals have become separated from what used to be social in education. Indeed, it seems like the public sector has come to fear what Pope John Paul II termed the "priority of the ethical over the technical" and the "primacy of persons over things" (Weigel, 1999, p. 23). This fear has translated into academic environments that further isolate students.

 ## Poverty and the Heart of Teaching

Many successful people grew up poor but were able to access support systems. Abraham Lincoln is one example. Poverty is a spiritual issue even more than it is a material one. Weak parental and weak school support can be devastating. Students from impoverished environments find that the farther they go, the more behind they get. Poor 4th graders, for example, are typically three grade levels behind their affluent peers. Half of these children do not graduate from high school. Schools need to recognize that their communities must be a family, especially to disadvantaged students.

Schools teaching to standardization without considering what really matters in children's individual lives are doing students and society a tragic disservice. Teachers are relaters when they care about the teacher-student dynamic, when they model an authority of family values as they respect the learner, when they are committed to the idea that learning and life at their deepest levels are relational, and when they invest themselves in a teaching model that includes spiritual goals. We have long accepted that values are better modeled than didactically taught. Socially we perceive that educators are committed to the value of relationships as we learn and as we live. But, do we realize that how we view human beings also makes a difference?

 ## High-Stakes Testing and Fear

U.S. public schools seem to march to a drumbeat of fear. Fear is an emotion wired into every human; the obsession with accountability certainly plays on that fear in schools and with teachers. Weeks before standardized tests are given, extra activities are put on hold in many schools across our country. These extra activities include recess time, field trips, and social studies and science lessons. During these weeks students perform hours of drill-and-kill test practice. One teacher told us that such an environment "constitutes her firing as a teacher." Many teachers do not feel trusted to perform their roles as professionals, fearing for their jobs if they take risks like providing recess or experiential education. The times demand the heart of the teacher-relater with the courage to stand up for the whole child.

. . . .

Relationships are important. It seems that teaching, more than any other profession, absorbs the day-to-day effects of societal dysfunction. Public school teachers are often scapegoats for learners' failures, even though they control few of the variables involved in a student's ability to learn. Teacher burnout is a reality. Half of all new teachers are leaving the profession in their first five years. Veteran teachers are questioning their reasons for staying in teaching as well. Forty percent of all teachers are discouraged with their jobs (Yarrow, 2009). One study (Marzano, Pickering, & Pollock, 2001) estimates that the teacher-controlled variables of instructional strategies, curriculum design, and classroom management account for only about 13 percent of the variance in student performance. Here is a fact that educators have always known: Great teaching comes from the inside!

 ## Sensitivity and Respect

The most challenging students serve as reminders that teaching is a call to serve learners as individuals. Michael Oher's biology teacher in the 2009 film *The Blind Side* took the time to learn who Michael was and how he was learning. Then she convinced some of her colleagues to do the same. Motivating students to believe in themselves and be inspired begins with whole teachers. Price (2006) says that "when students trust that a teacher authentically sees them as important, valuable, and intelligent people, they begin to respect and learn from that teacher, regardless of his or her color" (p. 126). Learners need the authority, sensitivity, and respect that the whole teacher brings to the classroom.

. . . .

Sensitivity is how human beings understand each other and thus themselves. It includes an understanding of the world of intentions, desires, and beliefs. We fail our students when we are insensitive to their values and cultural experiences. The ability to feel empathy is a highly valuable disposition for teachers and critical for the relater.

If we view students only as vessels to be filled with knowledge; if we treat learners as means to ends like raising test scores; if we play "gotcha games" through condescending approaches in teaching; if we fail to model values like respect, honesty, diligence, justice, and grace; or if we fail to honor learners' cultural beliefs and practices, we are guilty of displaying a short-circuited view of human beings and of teaching itself. What teachers believe makes a difference.

When teachers as relaters believe in spiritual goals, it makes a difference in practice. Relating spiritually to students is counter to the culture of those focused on competition and achievement or for those who fear spiritual goals. But the lack of an instructional belief system can contribute to disbelief in our students themselves.

Relaters: Believing in Students' Potential

Renowned Spanish Catalan cellist and conductor Pablo Casals wrote about the marvel of human uniqueness in *Joys and Sorrows* (1970), saying that "in the millions of years that have passed, there has never been another child exactly like you. You may become a Shakespeare, a Michelangelo, a Beethoven. You have the capacity for anything." Sensitive teachers know that their students are searching to find meaning and purpose in their lives, desiring to find it through opportunities to contribute to their world.

Spiritual goals can be met in the public schools by teachers who recognize the transcendent qualities of their students. Believing in our students does not necessarily require a religious persuasion, but it does mean that teachers can view their students as timeless, transcendent treasures. Plato, in *The Republic,* recognized this truth thousands of years ago: "The soul of man is immortal and imperishable." We teach not just a mind but a human spirit, an indestructible essence. As Dallas Willard (1998) has written, spiritual is what we already are, not something we must strive to attain.

Asserting that the human spirit can transcend the temporal seems to involve an intellectual risk for some scholars. Howard Gardner (1999) termed the human sense of the spiritual as existentialist intelligence in his theory of multiple intelligences. He found human spirituality less controversial as he applied the science of psychology:

With respect to such existential features of the human condition as the significance of life, the meaning of death, the ultimate fate of the physical and the psychological worlds, and such profound experiences as love of another person or total immersion in a work of art. (p. 60)

Gardner's conception of spirituality is broad and safe. We admire the emphasis on the relational aspects of spirituality. To believe in our students is to believe they can succeed, that they can be nurtured holistically to achieve their complete potential. Academic goals are always necessary in education. Our hope is to further clarify why belief in the indestructible spirits of learners is also vital. Serving something or someone beyond themselves is more than a desire for students; intrinsic in everyone is a belief and a need for action and commitment in their lives. Transformational teachers can nurture the concept that service above self ultimately helps students understand themselves and others. By looking outward to serve, learners can go inward to deepen into their education.

Antidote for 21st Century Schools

Valuing the holistic potential of learners can lead to other compelling conceptions of schooling. Education perceived as holistically transformational was hardly an invention of any group of *anno Domini* religious thinkers. Willard (1998) asserts that the goal of the teacher in ancient Israel was not to impart information, but to make a significant change in the lives of the hearers. Willard notes that it is a modern notion to bring people to know things that may not have an effect on their lives:

> In our day learners usually think of themselves as containers of some sort, with a purely passive space to be filled by the information the teacher possesses and wishes to transfer—the "from jug to mug model." The teacher is to fill in empty parts of the receptacle with the "truth" that may or may not later make some difference to the life of the one who has it. The teacher must get the information *into* them. We then "test" the patients to see if they "got it" by checking whether they can *reproduce* it in language rather than watching how they live. (pp. 112–113)

Transformational teaching might thus be seen as an antidote to an intense focus on informational teaching in modern education.

 ### Transformation of the Caterpillar

"Jug to mug" teaching is informational teaching. Somehow, despite all objective evidence to the contrary over the last century, this paradigm of pedagogy persists. Perhaps we have taken the wrong concept from nature, choosing the simpler act of an amoeba assimilating food over the more complex concept of transformation of the caterpillar into the beautiful butterfly. Learning is complex and beautiful. Let us embrace it as such.

William Butler Yeats said that "education is not the filling of a pail, but the lighting of a fire." Paradoxically one of the afflictions of our educational system is the intentional removal of information that is relevant to the real needs of learners. Essentialists may do it in the name of "back to basics" as they excise the humanities; politically correct educators may do it in the name of removing confrontational ideas that would offend a minority or interest group; and progressives may do it by removing language that would shed light on the truth of traditional values. Whole teachers can treat the afflictions in our educational system by kindling curiosity in learners within a supportive, nurturing context where controversial topics can be addressed. As teachers we need not be afraid of information, but we should fear those who would remove it or those who regard information as the end unto itself. How do we teach our students to think for themselves over a lifetime if they are not allowed access to ideas that they can consider, dissect, evaluate, adopt, or cast off, in whole or in part?

The clock ticks toward the expiration of relevant information sometimes before we teachers can give it or learners can convert it into knowledge, especially if the information is disconnected from the personal, individual experiences of students. Whole teachers who integrate social and spiritual goals with the academic will have more success in creating lifelong learners. Knowledge is remembered when it is personal, and knowledge is personal when holistic goals are met by whole teachers. Dockery (2008) asserts that without a sense of the sacred, all knowledge remains abstract. Unfortunately, we live in an increasingly abstract educational world, where social and spiritual development is often omitted from students' learning experiences.

The advances of the 21st century are happening fast, faster than even the most nimble of us often realize. Teachers as nurturers are an endangered species in this rapidly changing world. Perhaps we all should hit the pause button and reflect on what really matters in learning. Teacher heart and soul need not be left at the school door.

Why do we teach? This question is, among other things, a question that relates to cultivating richness in education. Why we teach cannot be answered without asking *who* we teach. It takes a whole teacher to develop the potential in our students.

Final Thoughts

A more traditional view of the teacher is of someone who knows and does. Such teachers are scholar-practitioners. But a classroom paradigm that begins with the learner, rather than the content, has implications for the role of the teacher. This chapter adds a third role, the relater, which creates a triad of roles played by a transformational teacher. It is the role most frequently ignored, forgotten, or misunderstood, but it is also the role that has often achieved the most lasting effects on students and their subsequent successes in life. Such a teacher establishes relationships that holistically impact learners. The relater role is not measured on standardized tests because it affects the social and spiritual aspects of life, and thus "only" indirectly affects academic education. The intersection of sacred and secular educational goals produces the vital concept of *calling* for teachers, which gives meaning and purpose to teaching, thus affecting students' lives. *Whole teachers* focus on relationships that foster connections to students' lives. It takes a whole teacher to teach a whole child.

3

TEACH THE
WHOLE STUDENT

The illiterate of the 21st century will not be those who cannot read and write, but those who cannot learn, unlearn, and relearn.

Alvin Toffler

The field of education needs transformational education with new urgency. Transformational education is a complete education, which means we teach the whole person. A seemingly quaint concept is this notion of teaching the whole child, for it begs the question whether we can teach part of a child. Oddly enough, many teachers do just that, and students respond accordingly—mostly or especially because of society's focus on academic performance and a corresponding distrust of education that defies measurement. Students need and want teachers to mentor them and to invest in them as complete individuals, not just as learners. We must demand both.

The *Whole Child Initiative* from the ASCD website (2010) describes the importance of teaching the whole person:

> The 21st century demands a highly skilled, educated work force and citizenry unlike any we have seen before. The global marketplace and

48

economy are a reality. Change and innovation have become the new sta-tus quo. A strong foundation in reading, writing, math, and other core subjects is as important as ever, yet insufficient for lifelong success. These demands require a new and better way of approaching education policy and practice—a whole child approach to learning, teaching, and com-munity engagement.

The Whole Child Initiative proposes a definition of achievement and accountability that promotes the development of children who are healthy, safe, engaged, supported, and challenged. We seek to redefine what a successful learner is and how we measure success. ASCD is helping educators, families, community members, and policymakers move from rhetoric about educating the whole child to reality. (p. 1)

Elliot Eisner (2005) raises the issue of the cultural problem as we face the dilemma of creating a more holistic environment in our schools. What can we do when society at large undervalues a whole child approach, opting for more uniformity and greater efficiency? He writes:

Can schools reflect "softer" values that substantially differ from the dominant cultural view? Given the fact that academic performance is key to social and economic mobility, can we expect people to take risks to enliven school life in non-academic areas when they fear it might com-promise their children's academic performance? (p. 16)

Teaching to holistic goals is risky—for some educators. Informa-tional teaching, for all its contemporary veneer, is the safer option because it connects to a past, known society in which schooling pur-portedly only addressed academic development. Great teachers, how-ever, have always inspired a holistic experience because they realized that narrow didactic teaching created learners with expiration dates, students who crammed for the final and had little desire or skill to continue lifelong learning.

Many young adults cannot tell you who delivered the Gettysburg Address, recognize words from the Declaration of Independence, or point to Georgia on a map. There is no substitute for learning basic skills, enforcing academic rigor, holding high expectations for learners, and measuring educational progress. Teaching students to simply recall content, however, can be a stupefying experience for both students and teachers. Remember actor Ben Stein's teaching tactics in the 1986 movie *Ferris Bueller's Day Off:* "Anyone? Anyone?" Content alone will not create passionate learners, nor will it develop students' sense of connectedness to the learning process or their communities.

High-stakes testing clearly has affected our school communities. The headline from a Tennessee paper proclaims "Snow days cause TCAP test worries for teachers." The reported concern of the superintendent, a whole child advocate, is that only 49 days remained before students were to take the Tennessee Comprehensive Assessment Program; canceling school meant giving up precious instruction time. The implication is that instruction is a means to a "new" priority in school, a battery of tests in the spring. A principal (Cheshier, 2010) is quoted about her nervousness over the loss of instruction time, saying, "I wish the state test was later. If we are going to be judged on what we've taught, we need to be given time to teach it." Like it or not, and most school people do not like it, a new informational education has been forced upon us. The greater sadness could be that educators, over time, might accept this educational outlook as right and good. Education centered on high-stakes testing has indeed become a race about who wins, and when.

Education should be about people. Investing in students is about relationships, and these relationships are complex and sometimes slow to develop. Whole child theory has always included physical, intellectual, and social-emotional dimensions of education. The social dimension should not be limited so that it excludes the potential of the human spirit. The creator of kindergarten, Friedrich Froebel, believed that children possessed "an interior spiritual force" that stimulated their self-activity. Maria Montessori (Murphy, 2006) expressed her famous method as having "discovered the world within the soul of the child" (p. 369). Education should include such attention to the human spirit. Inspiring relationships between teachers and learners can enrich and motivate the potential of the human spirit.

Investing in the Human Spirit

Seabiscuit is the story of a small-statured race horse who achieved nearly unbelievable success during the Depression. His owner, Charles Howard, made his fortune after changing his business from bicycles to Buicks in San Francisco. In the 2003 film, he offered a toast to his associates: "If we can start out there, and end up here, there is nothing we cannot do." These words can be applied not only to Howard's success in the car business but also to the men who owned (Howard), trained (Tom Smith), and rode (Red Pollard) the little horse. They worked together and believed in each other as much as they believed in Seabiscuit, accomplishing a miracle through hope, perseverance, and self-belief. In education, most pointedly in teaching disadvantaged students, "there is nothing we cannot do" when teachers buy into the human potential of their students. Loyal support for and investment in one another can achieve great things in the classroom, like motivation of the human spirit.

Motivating the Whole Learner

Pedagogy that inspires whole learners must come from teachers who are committed to the width of academic, social, and spiritual holism and the depth of motivating students to understanding the world around them. Depth in learning can lead to the gold standard in education: students who are less dependent on teachers for motivation and more dependent on themselves. The key to accomplishing this is interaction with a teacher who is both inspiring and intentional.

What keeps us from teaching the whole learner? Though many teachers already are committed to reaching the souls and minds of their learners, many others hold back from teaching holistically. Systemic pressure from state and federal regulations to teach to the test (so that students succeed on them) provides one answer. A self-induced pride of subject knowledge leads some teachers to think their single-minded focus is essential. Ironically, it is also easier to be a traditional, didactic teacher. It is ironic because political pressure leads many people to believe that standards call teachers to work harder. The opposite is true because informational teaching requires much less planning than transformational teaching.

Transformational teaching requires significantly more planning and a level of complexity that compels students to ask not just "What have I learned?" but also "Who am I becoming?" and "How does my learning affect my worldview?" Because fear is hard-wired into all our brains and can impede pedagogical responsibility, we are afraid to subvert teaching to standards by focusing more on meaning. Perhaps we are afraid that our peers will think we are undermining our commitment to academic knowledge when we reach for the more subjective dimensions of learning. We are afraid not necessarily of hard work but of the perception that such effort is superfluous. Perhaps most of all, we are apprehensive about crossing social boundaries with students and thus losing academic control.

Neurobiology can counter such concerns with a brain-based rationale. Social interaction is also hard-wired into the human brain, and learning is not meant to be an isolated experience. Teachers can create "communities of learners" (Collins, 2006) when they model high expectations and sensitivity for their students. Creating a community of learners intentionally fosters independent learning behaviors and develops a love for lifelong learning. The influential power of a teacher on the life of a student is unquestionable. As renowned linguist Frank Smith (1988) writes, children will learn to read and write if the people they admire read and write. One key to motivating students to deeper understanding is modeling a positive identity.

 A Student's Extended Family

A community of learners is best led by a transformational teacher who combines the power of deep content understanding with holistic learning. A wise and trusted teacher can be a mentor. Wisdom and trust matter in the education of the whole learner. There is a caveat, however. Not everyone is interested in education; or, at least many students have learned a certain indifference to school. Where do they learn this? "From parents" is one easy answer, but we should include "extended families" as we seek solutions: the television, motion picture, and music industries are part of a media family that bears responsibility. Schools and teachers must seek to be part of a village, an extended family, that rejects and/or is a conscious consumer of media. The mentoring of holistic learning is a family issue of spiritual courage.

Amy teaches in an alternative school in an urban school system. She is an experienced teacher with a deep desire to see her students succeed, which is the reason she continues to labor in what often seems a thankless environment. Holism in pedagogy is not a problem for Amy: Just yesterday she encountered a violent fight in the hall outside her classroom. Shaken but resilient, she was forced to recommend, along with her principal, separation from schooling for the adolescents involved. Amy cares about students in every way, including a tough love mentality when necessary. Amy is resilient because she looks for success one student at a time. She lives for the times that her alumni report on jobs gained and college degrees earned.

Education policymakers, administrators, and teachers are engaged in a battle for the minds of young students, resulting in the national effort to leave no learner behind. It is surely a worthy goal. We believe that the casualties in this battle, however, are not the intended states of ignorance but a whole generation of students. Ladson-Billings (2006) reminds us that the problem that teachers must confront in teaching disadvantaged students is not about what to teach. It is primarily about "how we think—about the social contexts, about the students, about the curriculum, and about instruction" (p. 30). She writes about what others have called the hidden curriculum: an education that takes place both inside and outside the classroom. Curriculum is what is learned whether the teaching was intentional or not. Students experience hidden curriculum, for example, on school buses and school hallways, learning "lessons" that educators may not have intended as part of the school culture.

Ladson-Billings's concern is for how we think about our students in terms of teachers' understanding of their school and nonschool cultures, and in terms of teachers' expectations. She asserts that teachers need to know that their students' identities are complex and have been critically shaped by their culture. "Whether teachers think of their students as needy and deficient or capable and resilient can spell the difference between pedagogy grounded in compensatory perspective and those grounded in critical and liberatory ones" (p. 31). Teaching the whole student requires that teachers understand the cultures in which they teach. Holistic education is grounded in students' cultural and socioeconomic realities. Teaching the whole person transcends the issues plaguing education reform. The Transformational Pedagogy Model represents a holistic expectation that students can achieve more in the process of learning.

Process of Learning: Strategic Learning Qualities

Teaching the whole child requires attention to content as well as to emotions and experiences. There is a focus on maximizing the potential of our students. The opportunity and time we're given to teach students demands a holism that includes content knowledge, a full range of social-emotional-spiritual competencies, and skills that allow students to learn independently, to adapt, and to self-regulate.

It is through process skills that students not only gain academic knowledge but also confront social and spiritual goals needed to be independent learners. The level at which students are beginning the process of learning is called readiness. Readiness is a lost concept in the era of accelerated curriculum. Many students of all ages just do not have the tools and the experience to respond successfully to the demands of mastering academic content and skills because they are not ready for symbolic thought.

 Promoting Readiness

Readiness can be imagined on a continuum with concrete thinking at one end and symbolic thinking at the other end. Solving problems at an abstract level requires skills built upon more concrete thinking. Such skills are developed through a process that should not be taken for granted. For example, most 6- or 7-year-olds are not developmentally ready for formal reading or for abstractions in mathematics. Indeed, most adolescents are not developmentally ready for symbolic thinking without concrete examples. To understand the concept of place value requires understanding of the more concrete pre-math skills of numbers, seriation, and counting. A foundation for whole learning must be laid by intentional teachers who "make a declaration of independence" for their students, who realize that most learners lack the process skills, the freeing how-to experience of learning. Students need explicit instruction or to be accorded the opportunity by teachers or parents in how to proceed.

....

Being an independent learner requires both desiring such a dimension of freedom and also knowing how to learn. Desiring independence comes from a pattern of success for the learner. The process of knowing how to learn is founded upon experiences that often involve trial and error. It may seem a paradox, but the best teachers practice a "controlled floundering" where students are allowed to explore and discover but also to succeed and fail within a supportive, caring classroom environment. Without the experience of failing, students cannot know success. Failing cannot be so profound that it leads to frustration and a lack of hopefulness in the learner. Students must be challenged at a level that is appropriate for their intellectual development. A transformational teacher recognizes when the signposts in student behavior point to frustration and intervenes.

Marcus teaches high school English in a magnet school through reading and writing projects that stress critical thinking and problem solving. He has found that test-prep practices form unnecessary barriers to the kind of authentic learning he desires. His students actually do better when they are free to concentrate on real-world skills of researching, constructing arguments, and presenting knowledge. During a project on *The Great Gatsby*, one of his students, Jerome, seemed highly agitated. "I do not see the point in reading an author [Fitzgerald] who is describing a fictional person who lived in the 1920s. I cannot relate to anything I am reading," Jerome confided. At that point Marcus realized that Jerome lacked the perspective and confidence that additional experience can build, so he decided to intervene.

He took Jerome aside and they studied one section from the novel together in which the author described Tom and Daisy as rich, careless people who destroy possessions and humans and leave others to clean up the messes. Marcus asked, "Jerome, what messes today are being left for future generations to clean up? Any ideas?" The question led into some issues in political science and biology. Making these connections allowed Jerome to trust the process of his learning more readily.

Strategic Learning Qualities

Teachers who trust the process of learning are successful in meeting the products of learning, which are learning goals and standards. For teachers to confront both depth and wholeness in their students' learning in an ideal learning environment, we propose the following *strategic learning qualities*. Teachers help to create more independent learners as a result of allowing students to develop these learning qualities:

• *Openness*—a quality that serves learners well in critical self-reflection on previous assumptions. Openness frees learners to discuss topics with other students, teachers, and other adults.

• *Skepticism*—an attitude that begins with openness and allows students to test and apply new perspectives through critical questioning. At its best, skepticism is a confident and humble search for the truth especially in the face of dogmatism.

• *Civility*—a quality that allows learners to respect fellow learners and teachers. It is a willingness to interact peacefully and collaborate with others in a learning environment.

• *Persistence*—an attitude tied to purpose. Learners persist with purpose despite obstacles. Teachers can encourage persistence by providing the needed learning resources and appropriate emotional support.

• *Imagination*—a creative spirit that reaches beyond the senses. It is an important quality because it takes learning from the objective to the subjective and back again. Albert Einstein said that "imagination is more important than knowledge" (Isaacson, 2007, p. 7).

• *Curiosity*—a quality that encourages learners to freely explore anything and everything. It is the trait that teachers must nurture passionately. Curiosity is a defining human quality.

Albert Einstein was well known for his imagination and curiosity. Isaacson (2007) reports on an invitation Einstein extended to poet Saint-John Perse. Einstein wondered how the poet wrote his poetry. "How does the idea of a poem come?" Einstein asked. The poet described the role played by intuition and imagination. "It is the same for a man of science," Einstein responded with delight. "It is a sudden illumination, almost a rapture. Later, to be sure, intelligence analyzes and experiments confirm or invalidate the intuition. But initially there is a great forward leap of the imagination" (p. 549).

To focus on the process skills that are strategic learning qualities is a focus on learning environment. Students who find themselves in inquiry-oriented environments, who are expected to use problem-solving skills, and who are asked to be more self-directed in their learning are able to develop these qualities. What is intelligence? Piaget perhaps had the most salient definition: the ability to solve problems. When students are asked to work hard and solve problems in a supportive environment, they develop these learning qualities; they deepen their understanding of content; they become more engaged with their work, which leads to more self-discipline; and they build a disposition toward lifelong learning. John Dewey in 1938 termed such engagement over a lifetime *continuity of experience*. To achieve the goal of independent learning for their students, teachers should be intentional in allowing them to develop these six qualities.

 Declaring Independence

In the Declaration of Independence, Thomas Jefferson made a case for natural rights, claims that cannot be separated from human beings because they are "endowed by our Creator." He enumerated three of them: life, liberty, and pursuit of happiness. What claims are natural and inalienable for education? One of them is surely the right to develop independence as a learner. How can teachers enable their students to declare independence? A short list would include teachers who

- Allow students controlled floundering with problems. Students learn by making mistakes in a supportive environment. Too much interference is over-teaching. Too little intervention is insensitivity. Teacher-relaters know the parameters and help their learners develop *persistence*.
- Encourage social interaction focused on inquiry learning. Students learn from each other as they share mutual learning goals. *Civility* is a quality that

students learn from practice under the eye of a caring teacher. The social interaction also must include teacher-student conferencing. Learners need the authority of their teacher to develop the confidence to be *curious, open,* and *skeptical.*

• Model a creative spirit by challenging students with great questions and challenging ideas. A compelling way to challenge students is to present short biographies of accomplished people past and present. Allow learners to be inspired and to be *imaginative.*

Encouraging self-directed learning requires more effort from both teachers and students than informational teaching. By their very nature, strategic learning qualities are learner-centered process skills and serve as an integral part of transformational teaching.

Recognizing Transformational Teaching

How can we recognize transformational education? When we walk into a classroom, there are three components on display: curriculum, teacher, and students. Each component should embed transformational teaching principles that reflect synergistic vitality.

• *Curriculum:* Is the content worth knowing? Is it important, inspiring, challenging, and useful? Not all subject matter is worth knowing—and we cannot know it all anyway. Does the information presented have application in society? Does it have meaning in the present lives of our students? Just because the information is old does not mean that a good teacher cannot speak it into currency. Does it seem likely that what is being taught will transfer effectively to the real world?

• *Teacher:* We talk of the whole child, but do you see evidence of a whole teacher, one who knows an academic domain, practices good pedagogy, and relates to the students? Does she respectfully connect the information to the learners by teaching through a cultural and individual understanding of the students? Is the teacher enthusiastic about her craft? Is there creativity and emotion in her teaching?

• *Students:* Are they using the strategic learning qualities, including openness, skepticism, persistence, civility, imagination, and curiosity? Are they engaged with learning and actively solving problems? Is there any evidence of learners' mirroring the teacher's healthy attitudinal qualities and values?

A Teaching Story

Consider the following story from a former high school English teacher in Mississippi. Does her subject seem worth knowing? Is Jane a whole teacher? Notice not only her inspiration but also her fostering of strategic learning qualities. Where can we observe them in her students? Notice also the development of a trustful mutuality that is a hallmark of a transformational teacher-student relationship and consider the questions in Figure 3.1, p. 64.

I was hired to teach Phase One English at Oxford High School in Oxford, Mississippi, as a first-year teacher. I had earned a bachelor of arts in English and secondary education from Ole Miss and had begun a master of education in reading, K–12. I had an exciting first year of teaching that had its peaks and valleys. Every teacher comes into her new classroom knowing certain things. In my case, and in those days, this is what I knew:

• Students were placed, according to achievement, in one of five phases for English and math. Phase Five students were high achieving, and course work was college preparatory. Phase One students were at risk academically and behaviorally.

• I was to teach them reading skills, five literary classics, grammar, poetry, and writing.

• In 5 classes, I would have 76 students, 7 girls and 69 boys. Five students were white; the rest were black. In all 5 classes, sophomores, juniors, and seniors were mixed.

• When discipline problems arose, students were to be sent to the office, where they were paddled with a large paddle.

• I had no academic materials suited for the students' reading abilities, which ranged from grade 3 to grade 9, with an average of reading ability at grade 5.

Here is what I did not know before I began teaching:

- Three veteran teachers had been hired to teach these classes, only to resign shortly.
- These students were friends and plotted to force me to resign also.
- The students discussed and compared what occurred in the individual classes.

What makes this a memorable anecdote is that I loved my first year of teaching and had a successful year. No one was sent to the office until April (and that was one boy who transferred to us from Phase Two in December). Although I was warned not to bring anything personal into the classroom or to have any decorations because they would be destroyed, over time, I was able to have plants, posters, bulletin boards, and personal items on the walls and on my desk. Nothing was ever destroyed. In fact, during the first quarter, the students started watering the plants, straightening up the reading corner, and cleaning out their desks.

At the beginning of the year, I made some bold announcements. I told the students that we would have bulletin board displays and that some of them would be for them to write on and others would be to match something we were doing academically, and that I would tell them which was which. I began the year with a bulletin board covered with white paper with the words "Welcome To and From" and sat a can of colored markers on a table nearby. They could sign their names to our "greeting card" if they wished. Everyone participated and checked it every day to see who had signed. Next, I announced that I was putting up a bulletin board that went along with a novel we would be reading. I told them that I didn't have much money and that I wanted to use the materials again. Not one mark appeared on that board, and nothing was destroyed. The remainder of the year, the bulletin board was changed regularly according to our study with "greeting card" boards interspersed according to holidays (Halloween, Thanksgiving, and all).

I also announced that we would handle our own discipline problems in our classroom, and that I had set a goal not to send a student to the office. In retrospect, that was not a wise announcement, but after about three weeks of students' "testing" me (laying condoms on my desk, using language to shock me, saying sexually suggestive things), they settled down, and we began making academic progress. I figured out that all classes were plotting these threats because each class did the same thing. So, I experienced the "plot of the day" five times. Later, the planning turned to comparisons of class activities to the extent that I needed to make certain we did the same thing in all five classes each day. The students didn't want to miss out on an activity. It made me plan carefully, so that what we did in the first class was successful because it needed to work four more times.

I also announced that we would be taking field trips, something else I was advised not to do. We had already gone on three field trips before the most memorable one happened. It was springtime, and we were going to read "A Rose for Emily," one of Faulkner's short stories set in Oxford. His grave was about three blocks from the school; so my plan was walk each class up the hill to the cemetery, go to his grave, and read aloud the first paragraph.

So on a beautiful Friday morning, the first class and I walked up the hill to the cemetery. I was talking about Faulkner as we entered the gate, only to have the entire class stop short of the cemetery because of the "haints," who they explained were ghosts. I didn't know what to do—that was my lesson plan for the day, and there were still four classes remaining. I finally persuaded them to walk to the grave with me by reading the paragraph outside the gate, which is what we did, except that they were in a tight bunch and pressed against me the whole time. The same scenario repeated for the next four classes, with the exception of the one student who refused to enter the cemetery, so I had another student stay with him by the gate.

When the rest of that class returned from seeing the grave, I noticed a pair of mockingbirds just inside the gate making a terrible fuss. They were flying from the tree to the ground, where their dead babies lay. The student who had refused to enter the cemetery—the one who had transferred from Phase Two in December—had killed them. As soon as we returned to school, I took him to the office—the only one that year.

A touching footnote to that memory is that after school that day, I was in my room grading papers. The windows were open, and I heard students calling me. Several boys, from different classes, told me that they had gone to the cemetery, gone through the gate, gathered the dead baby mockingbirds, and buried them. I cried. The following Monday, we had a good discussion about how precious life is.

According to the Phase One class proficiencies, I was to teach five classics: *The Scarlet Letter, Kidnapped, Treasure Island, Dracula,* and *Oliver Twist.* None of the students had the ability to read these classics; so I obtained condensed versions written at a low reading level from Ole Miss, and then read aloud selected parts from the classics. The students loved having me read aloud to them. In between the classics, I would read short stories and brief articles to them. Every day, when they entered class, they would ask, "Are you reading to us today?" My answer was always the same: "If you get your work finished." The result of that answer was no more tardies, attendance improved, and students monitored one another assuring the work was completed so I would read to them. During reading time, I always sat in a circle with them. I know that reading aloud to the students was the reason I was able to complete all the proficiencies for Phase One English.

I worried about teaching a unit of poetry because of my students' low reading scores and reading practices. Finally, one Friday in April I did a word association activity with them. I gave them 10 words and asked them to jot down the first thought that entered their minds. Nine of the words were pleasurable things—*picnics, swimming, football, music,* and so on. The last word was *poetry.* Not one positive comment was made about poetry; they wrote things like "yuk," "I don't like it," "I don't understand it," "I can't read it," or "I can't write it."

I told them that on Monday we were beginning our poetry unit, and I just asked that they keep an open mind. When each group entered the classroom on Monday, I had placed nature scenes all around the room and on the walls. The students were instructed to walk around the room and to jot down words or phrases or thoughts and sentences in reaction to the nature scenes. We used these as lines in poetry. When they returned to their seats, they selected their favorite lines. As a group, they arranged the lines in an order that would make a group free verse poem, wrote a bottom line that tied the lines together, and wrote a title. The poems were beautiful, and the students were amazed that writing poetry could be so easy.

Next, they wrote individual free verse. After that, I taught them to write structured poetry (haiku, tanka, syllable cinquain, and work cinquain). Then they were able to read and appreciate the poetry of some U.S. and English poets, including Robert Frost and William Wordsworth. The truly surprising occurrence was that after the poetry unit was concluded, they kept writing. They would carefully print or write their poems, mount them on construction paper, and hang them on the walls. They also shared them with one another.

It has been many years since my first year in that high school classroom, years that included a career in college teaching. My first year of teaching high school was not only exciting but a wonderful experience. I learned the importance of creating a safe, risk-free environment conducive to learning but also one where the teacher is comfortable to teach. I learned the power of reading aloud, power that transformed the students and me. And I learned the essentialness of trust to ensure that students will risk learning. (Story courtesy and printed by permission of Jane Anderson Scholl.)

Transformational Education

Where and how will transformational education take place in the future? Responding to the cultural needs of students with sensitivity is transformational. Demanding that students take responsibility for their learning is transformational. Teaching the whole person is transformational. Having high expectations of students with lifelong learning in mind is transformational.

Education grows out of the culture we create in our schools. Transformational teaching is focused as much on process as product because effective processes can create whatever product or outcome is desired. Teaching for coverage of content, for example, is rooted in the product culture of education, and developing strategic learning

FIGURE 3.1

Components of Transformational Teaching

Use this list of the classroom elements to help you identify components of transformational teaching in Jane Anderson Scholl's story and to consider how you use them in your own classroom.

Curriculum

What is Jane teaching that is worth knowing?

Give examples of pedagogy used that is inspiring and intentional.

What applications are evident to the world outside the classroom?

How does Jane use elements of traditional subject matter to connect to the real lives of her students?

Teacher

Cite how Jane exhibits whole teaching as a scholar, practitioner, and relater.

Does she respect her students as learners and as persons?

How would you rate her on an enthusiasm scale?

Where do you see creativity and emotion in this story?

Students

Give specific examples of where you see strategic learning qualities being evidenced by her students.

Are the students engaged with learning and problem solving?

Finally, identify an example of mutual transformation: How are the students mirroring Jane's attitudinal qualities and values?

---

qualities through thoughtful and inspirational teaching is rooted in a process culture in the classroom. When teachers do not know how or are unwilling to adopt strategic learning qualities for student self-direction and rigorous independent learning, they tacitly surrender to the popular focus on informational teaching.

Risk and Reward

Teaching for depth and wholeness has its risks and rewards. Transformational teaching involves a certain risk precisely because of its holism. Teachers must relinquish some control to allow students to self-regulate. To teach for change in students' lives requires knowing students and connecting to their experiences. Actor Dustin Hoffman provides one window into viewing transformational education.

In a television interview aired in 2006 on *Inside the Actor's Studio* he said, "Every art has its own failure quotient." Those who teach for a living understand this thinking.

 The Value of Failure

Hoffman's failure quotient means that trial and error are vital in the formative process of working with the humanities, the social sciences, the creative arts, and learning itself. Safe learning environments are responsive classrooms (like Jane Scholl's classroom cited earlier) that allow students to fall on their faces, pick themselves up, and learn from their mistakes without humiliation or total failure. As teachers we must ask ourselves, "What is my failure quotient for the learners in my classroom?" How much "failure" is allowed as students experiment with learning? The answer is just enough to lead to success.

We believe that schools are places where knowledge can transform lives. But lives are not transformed in schools that do not educate the whole person. Here we can learn from the past: Classical liberal learning was valuable in itself because it was intended to assist dialogue between knowledge issues and the improvement of human life in its totality.

Unfortunately, classical education has been disconnected from P–12 schooling and has affected many universities. There is an old story about a Vermont farmer and his wife driving down the road in their truck. The farmer's wife says, "Jeb, why is it that we don't sit close to each other anymore?" To which the farmer replies in his clipped New England way, "Bessie, ain't me that moved." The students have not moved, and much of the content has not moved either. But education has moved away from its holistic roots, and courage and persistence will be required of teachers who want to transform lives.

Final Thoughts

Teaching the whole person requires a commitment to a pedagogy of complete education, meaning that teachers teach toward goals that are holistic academically, socially, and spiritually. The strategic learning qualities can help teachers focus on the process skills needed for deep understanding, for transformation of the learner. Transformational education includes a reflective look at curriculum, teacher, and students. A transformational teacher is committed to the whole person as a learner. It is the teacher's role to prepare students' minds, and indeed their hearts, for a desire to discover more. Transformational teachers are needed to develop students' readiness to meet the challenges of the 21st century.

4

PLACE STUDENTS IN THE CENTER

Democracy requires of its citizens qualities that it cannot provide. Politicians can conjure an exalted vision of a prosperous, healthy, free society, but no government can supply the qualities of honesty, compassion, and personal responsibility that must underlie this vision.

Jürgen Habermas

Students belong at the center of our teaching pedagogy. Placing our subject matter in the center, which so many teachers do, fails those we intend to teach. When teachers aim too low with their expectations or mindlessly capitulate to the prevalent testing ideology, students suffer. Mindlessness is judging education's worth by relying solely upon objective measuring and remeasuring. Teaching to transform requires beginning with the learner and allowing ourselves to know just who it is we are teaching, including personality, ability, experience, culture, and aspirations. The act of teaching centers on a relationship. We must place students at the heart of our teaching.

Nancy, now a high school English teacher, shared a simple truth with us that indicates how teachers who know their students can influence them deeply. As a high school student, Nancy was the school newspaper editor. She spent a lot of time with the newspaper advisor and fellow student writers. They would piece the paper together in an old print shop, using scissors and wax as they attached the type to dummy boards. Losing one piece of paper was unacceptable. Nancy, ever the hyperattentive student editor, spied from the corner of her eye a scrap of paper fluttering to the floor and yelled, "Pick that up!" Her advisor chuckled good-naturedly, "Golly, Nancy, let it hit the ground first." To Nancy, now a teacher, it meant "don't borrow worry—let things happen and then make a plan for dealing with them." Nancy was profoundly influenced by this teacher who knew her and respected her as a learner and as a person. Nancy's teacher had the freedom to assess what matters. Nancy realized that her teacher had helped her learn the value of patience and planning through a prized relationship.

The connection between teachers and students is their relationship. How teachers view the students they teach makes a difference academically, socially, and spiritually. So, how do we perceive our students? Where do we "place" them? The list below offers teaching attitudes often displayed in classrooms:

• *Condescension:* a top-down, "I've got it and you don't" attitude, which originates in arrogance. Arrogance is selfish because it inhibits the development of a teacher-learner relationship. It proceeds from know-it-all hubris that has no basis in reality. In contrast, the act of teaching should develop humility within teachers. As we teach, we realize that the more we learn, the more we do not know.

• *Analysis:* "I will focus on the parts but not worry about the learning potential of my students." This view blossoms in outcomes-obsessed curricula. Analysis quickly loses track of the learner because of a desire to thoroughly isolate an objective, teach the objective, and assess the objective. Though contemporary standards are formulated to move learners forward, they can accomplish just the opposite: Students are lost in the effort to fulfill accountability standards. Analysis perceives students as consumers rather than the human resources they can be.

• *Entitlement:* "I want to find the smoothest route to accomplishing this job and being liked as well." This viewpoint flows from social and spiritual goals being allowed to trump academic goals instead of synergizing with them. The greatest risk taken by transformational teachers is to trust and respect learners because, like love, it makes teachers vulnerable to their students' wants and wishes and manipulations. Entitlement plays into students' worst attitudes—that they deserve an easy class, grading system, and path in life.

• *Compassion:* "I sincerely want to help students by displaying kindness and love even if it costs me." This perspective seems strongly spiritual—and it is. Compassion is displayed by teachers committed to holistic goals, and it doesn't come easily, usually growing in teachers bit by bit. It is a love tempered by disciplined focus on the real needs of students.

• *Synthesis:* "I see learners as more than the sum of some parts. I view them as needing a multifaceted approach to meet their needs." This teaching perception demands the greatest work in knowledge, attitude, and effort. Love is demanded, but understanding and empathy are also essential for synthesis. Its context is holistic and long-term.

Teachers may possess a combination of teaching attitudes. Teachers' dispositional orientations toward their students make a difference in the classrooms. They can shape what they teach and how they teach it. A caveat: While whom we teach takes priority in the Transformational Pedagogy Model, learner-centered classrooms must not compromise high expectations tied to what is taught. Placing students in the center of our pedagogy should include a deep commitment to the rigor it takes for them to reach their potential. These teacher views progress from extreme subject orientation to social sensitivity to spiritual understanding. See Figure 4.1 for an illustration of this progression.

Teachers need the spiritual authority that comes from respecting the learner. The teacher-student relationship is much like parenting, in that the relationship between parent and child is built on real love and born out of respect and trust. This mutual esteem ultimately makes the relationship work, whether it is in parenting or teaching.

FIGURE 4.1
Ways of Viewing Students

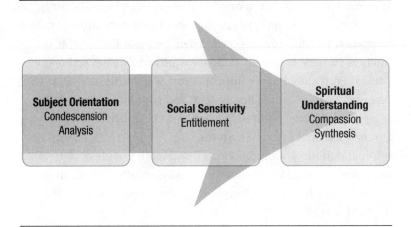

(→) **Even Selfish Attitudes Can Affect Others**

Abraham Lincoln, 23 years old, was asked why he was running for political office. He said that his peculiar ambition is to win esteem by rendering himself worthy of esteem (Goodwin, 2005). It is indeed an irony of life that our own attitudes, so selfish in tendency, are so instrumental in changing the lives of others. Teachers underestimate how they affect learners. Correspondingly, we often overestimate the importance of own knowledge. Wisdom develops when we realize the full dimensions of our roles in teaching.

Jackson (2009) relates a great story about Cynthia, her teacher-friend: Jesse, a particularly exasperating student, one day refused all persuasions to finish a makeup test. Refused, that is, until Cynthia offered to make him a peanut-butter-and-jelly sandwich. "Wasn't it just a bribe?" she was asked. Her answer: "You are missing the point. It is not the sandwich itself that matters. It's the fact that *I* make it for them" (p. 49). As a teacher-relater, Cynthia knew what Jesse needed. Her priority was Jesse. She started from where Jesse was because she knew him. She knew that his mother never took time to make her own child a sandwich. Once the student knew the teacher cared, he did the work. Creating relationships in which students believe that they are cared for is the foundation of transformational teaching. The dynamic of the relationship between Cynthia and Jesse is the key to academic, social, and spiritual transformation. The tragic short-sightedness of the Information Age is that the learner-centered class-room is a hoary issue undeserving of contemporary attention.

Mindful Teaching

Teaching has to be more than telling. It was Mark Twain who saga-ciously told us, "Teaching is not telling. If it were telling, we'd all be so smart we couldn't stand ourselves" (Wormelli, 2006, p. 3). Teach-ing is more than sharing the world of facts, more than information giving. To know our subject and to be articulate in communicating it is necessary, but not sufficient. Indeed, we all have experienced some effective teachers with a passion for and knowledge of their subjects who were less than sensitive to holistic needs. Many of us have learned to cope with teacher-scholars who epitomized strong disciplinary knowledge but were absent human attitudinal qualities. Some of us learn despite draconian teaching styles.

On the other side of the issue, a socially sensitive teacher-relater who is not deeply prepared in a discipline cannot be transforma-tional either. No amount of commitment to holistic goals can enable a teacher to overcome weak academic preparation or poor planning. The dualism of either/or continues to reign supreme in teaching: We gravitate toward the notion that we must choose between disciplin-ary dragons or permissive drones.

 A Culture of "And"

Teachers often exhibit the syndrome of either/or thinking. We dig in our heels faster than most, saying we cannot possibly teach this way and that we cannot teach that way either, because (1) we have never done it that way or never experienced it that way; (2) it doesn't make sense to us in the particular teaching style we inhabit; (3) we suspect or distrust the motives or thinking of the person who espouses this new idea; or (4) we hold to a combination of the above rationales. Why do we think like this?

Perhaps because we are so passionate about our work or because we are so obstinate about what we think we know. Wise counsel is to avoid the "divisive or" and embrace the "divine and" in human disputes (Trueblood, 1996). We should be thinking student and subject, whole learner and measured performance, scholar and relater, academic and social.

The act of placing the student at the center of pedagogical goals is controversial with many in academe. The dispute often comes from disciplines requiring students to master a hierarchy of factual subject matter, such as mathematics or science. Mastery in learning is a highly worthy goal, but it should not be a stand-alone pursuit.

Traditionalists are suspicious of any scheme that suggests subject matter is not the primary focus of education. *Suspicious* is the watchword because these same teachers think that a learner-centered classroom leads inevitably to less rigorous attention to the subject. Indeed, sometimes it can, especially when teachers weakly give in to a people-pleasing mentality. But there is no doubt that committed and active scholars often make great teachers; this occurs when their focus is on their learners as well as their academic domain.

 Pedagogy's Holy Grail

Many teachers readily buy into the dualism of either/or in education. One cannot possibly be learner centered and discipline centered at the same time, they contend. Content needs to be covered—in only so much time. Indeed, coverage and time are two of the flashpoints in talking about a more transformative pedagogy. Suffice it to say that the least difficult aspect of teaching is covering content. The holy grail of pedagogy surely involves a passion for the subject *and* the learner. Consider a teacher who can teach so that meaningful content is remembered and a student's life is transformed. Education is what we remember after we have forgotten everything we have learned.

The triad of scholar/practitioner/relater roles is an achievable goal for teachers. But how many teachers have worked with colleagues or been students of teachers who knew their subject but couldn't teach it? Those who believe that scholarship is sufficient in the classroom also tend to believe that presentation is the same as teaching. In addition, some have the notion that elementary teachers are great practitioners but do not need great scholarship. It is a mistake for teachers to be satisfied with fulfilling only one or two of the three roles. Ultimately, teaching for transformation is the individual responsibility of the teacher.

Consider middle school teachers. Even the most prepared and dedicated teachers of middle grade students can have difficulty occupying the mental and emotional landscape of pre-adolescent students. The teacher-relater role is crucial for middle school students, where socioemotional and academic needs abound, but where empathy often becomes a far-fetched notion for teachers. Knowing who it is we are teaching requires holism of roles as well as goals. Kate told us how excited and proud she was of her middle school learners who one day discussed the literature contrast in the transition from the Enlightenment to the Romance period. Later that day, she discovered her students playing "hangman" on the whiteboard. The epiphany for her was the stark contrast in her students between sophisticated adolescents and joyful, unpretentious children. Such a realization not only underlines the relater role but helps place and re-place students at the heart of our teaching.

Transformational teachers cultivate a curiosity that leads to scholarly work, indeed to lifelong patterns of learning. They also are relentless in finding a variety of ways for their students to learn, not being satisfied until their pedagogy connects with students. As relaters, transformational teachers have a "soft side" that leads to greater vulnerability. Experienced teachers know that soft must also be "tough," as in tough love when needed. Otherwise none of the teacher roles works.

Teaching is a moral, ethical relationship. Believing in learners means treating them as the ends rather than the means. If we are to be a friend to someone, for example, we love them for who they are, not what they should be. We treat a friend not as a means to get something for ourselves, but as an end, an entity deserving individual respect. The goal of people-focused teaching is to teach the student as an end, an individual with profound human dignity. On the other hand, the goal of achievement-oriented teachers who feel pressured by threats to job security is to serve their profession by teaching students to achieve better test scores, perhaps to the detriment of serving the ethical and social needs of students. The moral models represented by teachers are vital to strengthening character as well as a deep understanding of content and its implications in students. The moral development of learners is tied to good decision-making skills needed for upholding freedom in the face of unprecedented societal challenges.

 How Will You Be Remembered?

How can teachers in the public schools morally deepen their approach toward teaching and place their students in the center of what they are doing? One application of going deeper is a values-clarifying strategy, one that at first seems uncomfortable but is ultimately freeing in purpose: Secondary students can write their own obituary. In thinking about this assignment, learners realize their lives count in a spiritual dimension that transcends the here and now. They can also identify qualities they want to be remembered by. The teacher's role here is that of a relater.

Attitudinal Qualities

Placing students in the center of the classroom purpose requires that teachers first analyze their attitudes toward teaching, learning, and students. Attitude, or teacher disposition, occupies a part of the broad affective realm apart from teacher knowledge and skills. Contemporary scholars (Thornton, 2006; Tsui, 2009) have identified distinctive qualities of teachers that are critical to the development of teaching expertise, focusing on patterns of thinking and how teachers are disposed to act. Attitude is an academic, social, and spiritual quality that affects how teachers view their students. To assist us in exploring this paradigm, we reach for some classic work from a pioneer in the field of humanistic psychology: Carl Rogers (1969) identified three vital attitudes for effective teaching.

It was Rogers who introduced teachers as facilitators of learning into the educational lexicon. He was seeking a term other than *teacher* that would match with his concept of a teacher who had no intention of forcing anyone to know anything, a teacher who possessed three qualities vital to great teaching: realness, empathy, and prizing. Realness, or authenticity, characterizes teachers who are the same inside the classroom as they are outside. Teachers who inspire trust are real because their students can sense a purity of intention. Transformational teaching is not a performance but a relationship, and learners know that the teacher they see outside the classroom is the authentic person they see every day inside the classroom.

 ## Teachers Outside the Classroom

It is common for a student to spy a teacher in the supermarket or coffee bar and express surprise that the teacher "has a life" outside the classroom. Students often isolate their teachers to the classroom and school in which they serve. The surprise of discovering teachers in the real world—and the number of spies—can be minimized by teachers who make the effort to "get real." Be a real person with real emotions in the classroom; don't play the role of teacher as though it is an actor's part.

Empathy is differentiated from other dispositions through action. Empathic teachers view learners from the inside out. Empathy goes beyond sympathy by incorporating a willingness to walk in the learners' shoes. Empathic educators act in ways that are consistent with knowing students' identities. Empathic educators act in ways consistent with knowing their individual students, identifying and accepting learners' cultures and lives that include stresses of modern life. They support students as students seek to discover and understand their own identities.

Research suggests (DeWar, 2009) that empathy is a complex phenomenon involving a sense of self-awareness, taking another person's viewpoint, and managing your own emotional responses. It is helpful to think of empathy as an ability that can be developed with practice. To help students feel secure in the midst of instability and to recognize that we share a collective human experience are part of being able to empathize.

Delores is a veteran 6th grade science teacher. She has learned from experience and research that security and commonality are vital parts of teaching compassion. Delores developed a strong sense of empathy for her students' emotional security, often exploring negative emotions in a sympathetic, relational way. For example, she often asks her students, "How do you feel when someone was mean or indifferent to you?" Delores teaches empathy by modeling empathy. She looks for everyday opportunities to model empathy by focusing on what she and her students have in common with people who are victimized, whether they are found in literature, on television, or in their own neighborhoods. For example, Delores has discovered that making learners aware of connections to and similarities with the victims of Hurricane Katrina or the earthquake in Haiti helps motivate action that is rooted in empathy. It helps students react to the emotions of others and behave in kind and helpful ways.

Rogers's third attitudinal quality is distinctive because of its intense focus on individual differences. He chose the word *prizing* to express how the best teachers can make learners feel that they are unique prizes. Prizing transcends caring or kindness. This disposition in teachers, however, goes beyond teaching to individual differences, beyond differentiation to personalizing education. Prizing students represents the spiritual goal structure of the model where learners are treated as unique individuals, convinced that they are the special focus of their teachers.

 ## Mister Rogers's Neighborhood

Mister Rogers spoke to children like no one else. He knew his audience, and his intent was to communicate, not entertain. And Rogers communicated beautifully. Children ran to the television whenever they heard his quiet tenor voice singing the theme song. What was his secret? How could such an unassuming man, from his cardigan to his sneakers, be so successful with children? His touching and instantly classic interview with Jeff Erlanger, a child in a wheelchair, brought forth the best in Fred Rogers. The unrehearsed segment was a picture of sincerity, love, and honesty, not pity. Rogers *prized* Jeff when they sang together "It Is You I Like." He showed daily how much he liked children. Perhaps Rogers's greatest contribution was the distinction he made between reality and fantasy. His puppets and props engaged children in a world of fantasy. But Rogers always took the kids on the trolley car back to reality. The show always seemed to end on a note of emphasis of individuality: "There is no one exactly like *you*, never has been, never will be."

....

Prizing is the quality that connects. It has such a strong influence that it alone can infuse a sentiment that a certain teacher made a permanent difference in a student's life. Just as teachers' attitudinal qualities make a difference in holistic learning, learners' attitudinal qualities are vital in learning.

Education can benefit from a reconnection to learners and their holistic needs. Ensuring that all students learn connects to a fundamental democratic ethic. Human life is precious and worthy of nurturing. Because of this belief, a nurturing pedagogic dynamic would naturally be the foundation of our educational system as long as we also realize that individualism has its limits.

Attribution Theory

Sensitive, nurturing teachers affect the performance of their students in ways that transcend the academic. It is vital that teachers know themselves because what they believe makes a difference in student beliefs. Educational psychologists term people's beliefs about what causes success and failure *attributions*. Attributions include such things as effort, ability, luck, task difficulty, mood, physical appearance, and teachers' or peers' behaviors (Schunk, 2008). Interestingly, learners' perceptions of themselves relate to attributions as strongly as they relate to reality. Perceptions often become students' personal reality. Learners sometimes attribute causes of events to factors within themselves, such as lack of ability or work ethic. Ormrod (2004) and Weiner (2000) term such perception *internal locus of control*. Factors attributed outside themselves like good luck, an accident, or even other people's frowns are examples of an external locus of control.

 Attributional Style

A similar psychological term is *attributional style* (Ormrod, 2004). Learners can assume a mastery orientation, in which they believe they can do it, or they can adopt an attitude known as learned helplessness, believing they cannot do it. Those with mastery orientation as a style do better in the classroom and on the athletic field. Success breeds success, and failure develops a learned helplessness, especially when the perceived cause is outside the individual's locus of control. Teachers can make a difference in their students' attribution styles, in what learners think about themselves, and thus in how well they do in the classroom.

Placing students in the center of our teaching philosophy leads to transformational learning. Transformational learning feels like an epiphany for the learner. To be suddenly transformed by the confidence of knowing, to realize that hard work in reading and studying has been rewarded, to bask in the approval of a trusted teacher, to suddenly desire to know more and seek knowledge individually are all epiphanies of transformational teaching. Great teaching involves an energizing dynamic between teachers and learners.

We use the term *teacher-learner dynamic* in the profession because of the energizing, synergizing, and changing nature of the relationship between teacher and student. As teachers, we make many decisions while interacting with variables that include the procedural, such as planning and assessment; the theoretical, such as cognitive or behavioral perspectives; and the instructional, which encompasses the learner's needs and motivation. Transformational teaching is dynamic and complex.

 ## Flow

Psychologist Mihaly Csikszentmihalyi (Gardner, Csikszentmihalyi, & Damon, 2001) would remind teachers that doing fulfilling work feels good. He says that with the right environment (clear goals, immediate feedback, challenge level to match skills) "we have a chance to experience work as 'good'—that is, as something that allows the full expression of what is best in us, something we experience as rewarding and enjoyable" (p. 5). He famously termed this concept *flow*, which he defines as highly enjoyable human moments where we can be lost in seemingly effortless performance. Achieving flow is a worthy goal in teaching and learning, especially as it relates to the dynamic relationship between teacher and student.

Service Learning

Thinking about what matters is valuable, but taking action steps enhances academic, social, and spiritual understanding and self-fulfillment. The strategy that connects learners to meaning and purpose is service learning. Service and learning should be joined in a goal structure in the classroom. Although participating in a school community service program is valuable and indeed beneficial, the benefits of the service rendered can be lost if it is not connected to learning objectives set by the teacher as part of a required curriculum. No greater application exists in a transformational teacher's repertoire. Service learning embodies the synergy among academic, social, and spiritual goals in the Transformational Pedagogy Model. Nothing embodies a student-centered teaching paradigm better.

> As teachers, we can affirm this soulful dimension of youth culture. Examples of altruism and activism from popular culture can provide a bridge from alienated adolescents to connect with their own yearning for finding meaning through service for others. Instead of judging and distancing ourselves from popular youth culture, we can support this expression of soul in our students by naming and honoring it whenever we see it. (Kessler, 2000, p. 71)

Service learning allows for diverse expression of sociocultural beliefs. We live in a time where incorporating diverse perspectives in the classroom is vital. Now is the time to reintegrate social and spiritual aspects of education in public school classrooms by encouraging service in classroom goals. Diversity finds its fullest meaning in service to others.

 Service and Meaningful Learning

Deborah teaches students from low-income families and has learned that her students often lack confidence to perform in competitive classroom environments. She has discovered that her students thrive in cooperative classroom environments that foster service to others. Deborah's students serve in area food relief ministries where they can connect to lives outside school and bring back to her classroom stories of resilience and accomplishment. Her service learners write about their experiences and share their writing with classmates and with other classes in the school. Building relationships inside and outside the school with the support of an adult anchor like Deborah fosters meaning and engagement in the lives of her at-risk students. Deborah embodies and synergizes the scholar, practitioner, and relater roles in teaching.

....

Unfortunately, classrooms have become increasingly dogmatized. Rule making and rule following dominate classroom climates, taking the focus off teaching the whole child. Nel Noddings (2005) observes that even when teachers "recognize that students are whole persons, the temptation arises to describe the whole in terms of collective parts and to make sure that every aspect, part, or attribute is somehow 'covered' in the curriculum" (p. 12). Students are more than a sum of parts. Pedagogy should include a synergy of the model's goals, leading to valuing the uniqueness of students as whole learners, individuals who deserve special respect at the center of our teaching efforts.

Why do we teach? The answer of course involves who we teach. We teach for learners, not only to meet their academic needs but to transform their lives. Alexander (2006) comments on the academic reality that some learners begin their journey with limited cognitive and motivational resources, while others are building on rich resources they already possess. To face this reality, teachers should not "unintentionally contribute to the problem by overlooking what students do know or by presenting them with educational tasks that are ill-suited to their abilities or needs" (p. 82). Sensitive teachers who place students in the center of their pedagogy can recognize the difference between a challenge and a frustration for students.

Final Thoughts

This chapter describes why it is vital to place students at the center of teaching. The relationship between teachers and learners is the dynamic that makes learning happen. Planning and organizing for instruction requires an understanding of students. Pedagogy then becomes less about what the teacher would like to teach today and more about what will cause learning to take place. How we perceive our students is a starting point for transformational teaching. Indeed, our democratic system demands the fundamental ethic of nurturing individual learners. Psychological concepts like dispositions, locus of control, and attribution style are important for teachers to consider because they make a difference in how well students perform in their classrooms. To really change our schools, we have to proceed with deeper convictions about the needs of those we teach. Connecting to the experiences of the learner is the starting point for pedagogy. To teach to transform, we must shed our dualistic tendency of thinking we cannot teach our subject well when we place learners at the heart of our teaching.

part
TWO

Children are problem solvers and, through curiosity, generate questions and problems: Children attempt to solve problems presented to them and they also seek novel challenges. They persist because success and understanding are motivating in their own right.

Bransford, Brown, and Cocking, 2000

5

TEACH FOR LEARNING

The reasonable thing is to learn from those who can teach.

Sophocles

We teach to change the learner, and we have not taught unless learning has taken place. Unless we begin with expectations related directly to the learner, instead of the teacher, we will delude ourselves in the classroom. Teachers can walk away from a presentation or other classroom experience and say, "Wow, I was great today! The words came easily, and the student response was so energizing. I really taught today." Alas, a short quiz or discussion reveals that the students did not understand or learn at all.

Teaching can occur without learning—it is an empirical fact that two people are involved and that each teacher and learner is usually doing something different. Leamnson (1999) says that "teaching is done *by* someone, and not *to* someone" (p. 53). Teaching, especially if it is to be transformational, must be more than presenting. The semantics make a difference. Teachers know from experience that there is no necessary relationship between what is taught and what is learned. The mystery is in the dynamic of connection, not separation. The connection between teaching and learning is a transformational concept, supported by the academic-social-spiritual connection between teachers and students. How we conceive of the transaction between teacher and learner matters very much.

Barr and Tagg (1995) differentiate between an instructional paradigm and a learning paradigm. For example, an instructional paradigm views knowledge as existing "out there," while the learning paradigm sees knowledge as how our individual experience shapes it. If our mind-set is instruction, we place subject matter first in classroom priorities and worry about standardized outcomes. If we place the learner in the center of our pedagogical paradigm, we care not only about outcomes but about individual growth in all its dimensions. When teachers focus on a learning paradigm, they use connections between content and student experiences to make learning meaningful and personal. Because emotionally engaged learning is more memorable and powerful than cognitive learning alone, the learning paradigm offers a more holistic approach to instructional methodology.

 ## The Purpose of Standards

As states surge toward common academic standards, many think that we should identify subject matter related to standards, and then teach it. We think this is misguided. Standards should be seen as guides or structures that give teachers launching pads for creativity and for connecting to the individual experiences of learners, as they are teaching their subject. If we keep the uniqueness of each learner firmly in mind, we will not surrender to the fallacious thinking that we teach something "out there" instead of knowing that we actually are teaching something "in here"—our students.

Connecting teaching and learning is an extension of the teacher-student relationship. Teaching can occur without learning. It often does! Teaching for learning, however, requires commitments from the teacher and the learner. The teacher commits effort and a belief in students' abilities; learners commit effort, openness, and a desire to succeed.

Teachers must practice diversified teaching strategies by being willing to explain and present concepts in several ways in an effort to reach each student. Varied instruction is part of a strong teaching repertoire. Teachers must also rely on trust in the classroom—guiding students through difficult processes requires trust. Students must be willing to be occasionally uncomfortable while learning. Transformational learning sometimes feels like a painful stretch on sore muscles. Students must be willing to engage the edge of this cognitive discomfort, supported by the encouragement of their trusted teachers.

Understanding Teaching and Learning

Today's students need an extraordinary knowledge base and the process skills to find and use relevant information. They also must evaluate that information with a value system attuned to social and ethical service. Because technology is sure to continue to modify human experiences, we cannot depend on the past or the present for our knowledge base. But we can depend on the fact that learning is unique to each person and should always be our focus in teaching.

Few would argue with mastery of the basics with their attached outcomes, or with respect for genuine authority, or with disaffection for a permissively soft pedagogy where learners are unaccountable. However, we confuse the necessary with the sufficient in education. The goal should not be essentialism of information but the timeless educational goal of transformation.

Teachers are pressured to get on board with the latest curriculum emphasis, which might have been multiple intelligences, direct instruction, the latest reading program, or differentiated instruction. Although there is nothing wrong with new ideas or new approaches to teaching, the district attitude is often an exclusive one: The new program must supplant everything else. Tried and true pedagogy or curriculum is out; the new one must replace it. Such limited vision is discouraging and harmful to teachers and students. What is proven or timeless is often ignored or must give way to the latest and greatest. We emphasize the teaching of content but ignore process skills like critical thinking. We teach basic skills of reading and math while we demote social studies and science to the "if I have time" bin of teaching priorities. And we focus exclusively on academic goals to the steady demise of the social and spiritual goals.

Jolie Lindley (2010) is a high school teacher who teaches for learning. Being a whole teacher to whole learners seems second nature to her. Her issue, however, is why there is a systematic effort to pay her more for teaching to test scores. She wants to be paid more for extensively planning lessons, staying after school to grade papers, paying her own professional development expenses and for teaching supplies, communicating regularly with parents, and making her classroom a safe and caring environment where her students feel secure. Jolie has her students' learning in mind, investing in them academically, socially, and spiritually by putting her life and soul into the profession.

Though the learner is in the center of the model, transformational teaching informs the teacher's behaviors and beliefs. Leamnson (1999) observes that the teacher's

> classroom persona is important because that's the entity that students encounter. How students feel about a teacher has, for good or bad, a powerful influence on how they listen, whether they work on course content, and how much they learn. (p. 71)

Transformational teachers recognize their role as moral agents who confront problems and who desire transformation of their students, of their community, of their world. They desire an intellectual conversion of novice learners to more expert learners. For learning theorists (Bruning, Shaw, & Ronning, 2004; Schunk, 2008), the distinction between expert learners and novice learners lies in the realm of problem solving. Experts have a high competency level in problem solving, and novices are learners who have some knowledge but perform poorly in problem solving.

 Connect and Transfer

To confront a problem generally requires transfer of learning where knowledge is applied "in new ways, in new situations, or in familiar situations with different content" (Schunk, 2008, p. 209). The confrontation and transfer can be academic, social, and spiritual in context. Not many could have predicted the credit crisis in fall 2008 where trusted financial institutions failed or were salvaged by the U.S. government. The dimensions of the problem are staggering both analytically and morally. It is essential for transformational learning that learners first confront new knowledge with the guidance of their teachers, then analyze, synthesize, and demonstrate their new perspectives in their own language.

....

Contrast this transformational role with the more common informational teaching. Information is defined in various ways, but it usually refers to a kind of disaggregated knowledge, or a collection of facts and data. We would emphasize the latter definition and clearly separate the two: Information is a set of facts or data presented, and knowledge is information that has been learned. Great presenters of information are not necessarily great teachers.

Informational teaching is focused on imparting information, taking it from books and depositing it in students' minds. An informational pedagogy model places the teacher as "sage on the stage." While listening to a great lecture will always be valued, schooling tends to be too much about the teacher or the knowledge taught.

The 20th century model of pedagogy (Sawyer, 2006) was designed around transmitting knowledge to learners and then testing them for that knowledge. This ideology has only accelerated in this century into informational teaching. Learning as a concept and process, as a guiding force, takes a backseat. Sterilized, disembodied, nonrelational teaching to standards and tests that excludes students' motivational fire, needs, and interests is inadequate when the goal is to teach for learning.

Starting with Our Students

Consider one teacher's predicament in trying to teach for learning. Tameka works in a large urban school district where many schools are failing to meet Annual Yearly Progress (AYP) goals. The district, in its effort to provide instruction attuned to the needs of students who struggle with reading, has mandated computerized reading programs that require students to sit in front of computers for hours each day. Tameka feels, along with many of her colleagues, that instruction and assessment have been substituted for teaching and learning. She longs for the personal, one-to-one and small-group contact in which her students can interact. Such personal attention would allow her to devise formative assessments of her students' reading progress. While the district programming may be well intentioned, the priorities seem focused on instruction rather than on learning.

If we understand how students' learn, we will be compelled to equip ourselves with effective pedagogies based upon the best research in learning and human development. During the last decade, a scientific revolution has occurred in cognitive learning theory. Our understanding of how the human mind works is more complete now than it has ever been.

 Activate Prior Knowledge

David Ausubel wrote in his 1968 textbook *Educational Psychology: A Cognitive View*, "If I had to reduce all of educational psychology to just one principle, I would say this: The most important single factor influencing learning is what the learner already knows. Ascertain this and teach him accordingly" (as cited in Shulman, 1999, p. 39). Robyn Jackson (2009) restates it as one of her learning principles: Start where your students are. When learning theory and research are joined with the goal of nurturing the intellectual and social potential of students, transformational teaching becomes focused on learning.

The act of teaching loses effectiveness when priorities are skewed and when the process of learning is misunderstood. Priorities are misplaced when either the curriculum or the teacher is placed at the center of the model's center instead of the learner. Students shoulder the blame for our teaching woes, labeled as "bad students," as per Postman and Weingartner's (1969) classic analogy of doctors in a hospital who blamed their patients' untimely deaths on "bad patients." These doctors were convinced, in a darkly humorous way, that their medicine was good in itself. Jerome Bruner (1996) identifies such a didactic bias when a teacher

> views the child from the outside, from a third-person perspective, rather than trying to "enter her thoughts." . . . In such a regimen, if the child

fails to perform adequately, her shortcomings can be explained by her lack of "mental abilities" or her low IQ and the educational establishment goes scot-free. (p. 56)

Part of the transformational experience in pedagogy is achieving a first-person perspective, looking through the eyes of students by reconstructing their points of view: informed empathy in action. To understand transformational teaching, we must understand the learning process, but we also must understand our students. Growth as a teacher requires shedding our tunnel-vision tendencies that view the learner solely through academic eyes and that assert only one best way to teach. Teaching is as individual as learning and learners.

Myths of Pedagogy

Given that pedagogy focuses on the interaction between academic disciplines and social beings with diverse needs, it is understandable that a certain mythology has developed around teaching and learning at all levels. Bruner (1996) writes about these myths, identifying them as *folk pedagogy*. He observes that laypersons and teachers often use everyday intuitive theories about how other minds work, about how people learn, and about how teachers should teach. These myths are convenient fiction, often half-truths that play into educators' ideologies. See the myths as disputed by the realities (facts) in Figure 5.1.

Bruner's concept includes a variety of assumptions about children: They are willful and need correction; they are innocent and need protected from a vulgar society; they lack skills and need practice; they are empty vessels and need to be filled with the knowledge adults can provide; they are egocentric and need socialization. Bruner insists that a culturally oriented cognitive psychology need not reject use of folk pedagogy as mythology because, even if the assumptions are wrong, they still have an enormous impact upon teaching. Teachers need good theory and research to guide their practice.

Transformational pedagogy requires that learning be the goal of teaching because the ultimate reward is the learner's transformation.

FIGURE 5.1
Fact Versus Fiction

Myth	Fact
Blank stares and bovine-like eyes on student faces are inevitable and unavoidable; teach expecting to see them.	Human curiosity is a natural gift. Curiosity can be rekindled and nurtured because learners are competent, active agents in need of the support of teachers and other learners.
Lectures, even well-planned ones, dampen enthusiasm for learning.	Students lack knowledge and can benefit from teachers whose lectures connect to their individual experiences.
Effective teaching occurs in direct proportion to time on task.	The quantity of time spent on learning content or skills is an unreliable variable in itself. While time can be an important element in learning, the key to effective teaching is usually the quality of the time (i.e., how engaged the learner is with the subject matter).
Teaching someone something adds to their storehouse of knowledge.	Teaching is more than telling someone something new. Teaching occurs when learning happens, and learning results when students are engaged with new information in contexts meaningful to them.
Tests contribute to the learning process because they show what the students have learned.	Exams hold students accountable and can give important feedback that reinforces learning. Learning, however, is only demonstrated in the students' ability to apply their new knowledge in different contexts.
The best teachers are those teachers with a reputation for being hard.	Rigor is good when it means maximum, meaningful learning. Rigor is bad when it means excessive and irrelevant requirements for the learner.
Teachers with a reputation for making learning "fun" have sacrificed standards.	Emotion is a basic human structure connected to learning. The best teachers find ways to incorporate joy in learning.

FIGURE 5.1
Fact Versus Fiction (*continued*)

Myth	Fact
Twenty-first century technological advances are demonstrating how less than essential teachers are.	Students need teachers' assistance in learning. The process of learning requires the organization, insightful challenges, feedback, and motivation provided by good teachers.
The traditional role of a teacher, to cover essential subject matter, is vital.	Teaching in the traditional sense is vastly overrated. Learners often learn despite unnecessary emphasis on coverage, finding such teaching mostly irrelevant.
Most adolescents are ready for symbolic thought and higher-order reasoning.	Half of college freshmen have not reached this formal stage of cognitive development. The most effective teachers take this research into account and otherwise plan for concrete-thinking students by fostering interaction between students and their physical environment, between students and others (including teachers and peers).

Source: From "Debunk these 10 myths about teaching and learning" by T. Rosebrough in *The Teaching Professor.* Copyright 2003 by Magna Publications. Adapted with permission.

Placing students in the center of our teaching paradigm is an important step in knowing them. Respecting the learner establishes not only a mutuality of trust, but also the obligation for teachers to understand how their students learn. Understanding the myths of pedagogy leads us closer to the goal of teaching for learning.

Final Thoughts

We have explored placing learners and their needs at the center of the teaching model. Teaching is about knowing who we teach. Knowing the audience is important because we have not taught until they have learned. Teaching is more than telling, and covering curriculum and standards is the least difficult aspect of teaching—albeit impossible in the time afforded to teach in schools (Marzano & Haystead, 2008, p. 7). We introduced why it is so important to know how learners learn. When we know how students learn and engage them in their learning, they begin to take some responsibility for their own learning. Engaged learners are self-regulated, defining their own learning goals and evaluating their own achievement. They become energized by their learning; their joy of learning leads to a lifelong ability to solve problems by transferring their knowledge to new contexts. Engaged learners are also collaborative, having and valuing the skills to work with others. This chapter concludes by challenging teaching's conventional wisdom with facts of pedagogy.

6

KNOW HOW
STUDENTS LEARN

Mr. Gradgrind in Charles Dickens' Hard Times *has become a model of the worst sort of teacher perceived as cold, aloof, sterile, obsessed with pounding facts into the heads of reluctant students. Indeed, the term* grind *has entered the lexicon to describe a bad or difficult school (or work) experience. Mr. Gradgrind severely criticized a student for not knowing the dictionary definition of a horse, despite knowing all about horses from her home experience. The overriding concept is that of a teacher who is out of touch or without interest in students' personal lives, attitudes, emotions, or motivations.*

Pulliam and Van Patten

It was prophetic of Mr. Gradgrind to be teaching about horses. In the profession of education, we spend most of our time putting the cart (knowledge) before the horse (learner). But if we are to be transformational teachers, the horse that is learning must pull the cart of teaching. As teachers, we must know how our students learn.

Teaching should be about transforming learners through a synergy of academic, social, and spiritual goals. How do teachers create that synergy? How can teachers affect the transformation of learners? This chapter focuses primarily on the practitioner in the Transformational Pedagogy Model, who specializes in knowing how students learn and chooses the best pedagogies accordingly. We begin with explanation and elaboration about how learners learn.

Teachers must be experts on learning. Much effort is typically expended in education training programs on teaching methodology. Amazingly, little energy is expended on understanding the process of learning. It is a common misunderstanding that we can teach without knowing how learners learn. This misunderstanding probably flows from a misconception of why we teach. Too many teachers are in the profession for the wrong reason, as exhibited by too many teacher-centered classrooms focused on presentation of information.

Good teaching demands that we use our heads and hearts. We employ our minds to understand how learners learn, how we might differentiate our pedagogical approaches, and what *must* be taught. We use our hearts to understand why we are teaching, to create a classroom environment that prizes learners individually and personally, and to instill confidence in students that they can be transformed by the experience of learning.

Teaching Challenge

Yvonne knew she was a demanding history teacher who often inspired productivity in her students. But Edwin was a different case. Edwin seemed to have a streak of independence that resisted his teacher's motivational efforts. The more Yvonne pushed, the more Edwin resisted. She began to realize that his fear of failure was not as strong as his desire to demonstrate his autonomy. In the middle of a lesson on the end of the Cold War in the United States, Yvonne huddled with her recalcitrant student. "If you can figure out a different way to show me you know this material, I'm willing to look at your idea."

To borrow a phrase, the rest was history. Edwin began to thrive as a creative, divergent learner. His learning response often was musical, and it was always reflective. Yvonne's colleagues also noticed the change in Edwin and asked Yvonne what she had done. She shared, "I realized that the best way to show Edwin I cared about him was to provide learning options for him. I realized I owed him that respect." This teacher used her heart as well as her head. Respecting the student requires that teachers approach their craft from the perspective of the learner. This is the ultimate challenge for anyone that teaches.

Informational teaching and learning are part of the fabric of contemporary culture, and they seem to be dulling many students' perceptions and understandings of their world. Nicholas Carr (2008) addresses an underlying philosophical issue of our time by asking, "Is Google making us stupid?" The worry is that the Internet invites a blurred distinction between the surface nature of information and the deep understanding required for knowledge.

Mark Bauerlein (2008) expresses the concern that digital culture has changed the way students learn, but at the expense of literacy and cultural awareness. He believes that misuse and overuse of the Internet crowds out vital knowledge and values of citizenship as young learners immerse themselves in video games, cell phones, laptops, and blogs. Teachers do not wish students to forsake these remarkable, accessible research tools, but they worry that students are becoming overly self-absorbed in the digital culture. Self-absorption and the time often spent on electronic pursuits have critical educational implications.

The digital culture offers a temptation to many learners that is rather irresistible: Plug in and tune out. While it is certainly true that many digital learners are more connected globally, it is ironic that the most connected generation in history also demonstrates tendencies to be the most disconnected learners educationally, culturally, and emotionally. Don Campbell (2008) writes

> The Internet has moved knowledge from the brain to the fingertips: Who needs to know about Impressionism or Charles Dickens or George Washington Carver or . . . even George Washington? Why carry such information around in your head when Google will deliver it in seconds? (p. 11A)

A spike in connectivity seems to be occurring as many students, especially urban and minority, are disconnecting from school. Students are quite vulnerable to a shallow, fingertip understanding of knowledge and culture—a perspective of which learners in any century are often unaware until challenged. Adolescents often lack the sophistication and decision-making skills needed to be conscientious consumers of information. Students need, as we shall see, the profound social support of adults in their learning environment to "put it all together."

Informational to Transformational Learning

For learning to be transformational, it must yield more than students' adding or assimilating new information into an existing schema (Piaget, 1969). The process that Piaget describes as accommodation involves changing existing schemata or adding new ones. For example, a child has a "comfortable" schema for horses until one day she sees a Great Dane. A parent says, "No, that Great Dane is a very big dog, not a horse. Dogs bark and horses neigh." The child now has to change her horse schema and add or change a new dog schema. Such change is what we call learning. This description of learning is informational in its essence. It is based on learners encountering discrepancies in their objective learning environment and making sense of them. Piaget also described a similar process for moral and cognitive development. Exposure to moral dilemmas in our learning environment can challenge existing schemata, which in turn leads to moral and social growth.

Informational learning environments can become transformational. The 21st century demands learning skills and dispositions that can adapt to new situations and environments, to solving problems that heretofore did not exist. Zakaria (2006) writes about an interview he held with the minister of education of Singapore, the country that was sitting atop the global science and math rankings for schoolchildren. He asked the minister:

> How [can you] explain the fact that Singapore has few "top-ranked scientists, entrepreneurs, inventors, business executives, or academics [while] American kids test much worse in the fourth and eighth grades but seem to do better later in life and in the real world? (p. 37)

The minister of education, Tharman Shanmugaratnam, answered:

> We both have meritocracies. Yours is a talent meritocracy, ours is an exam meritocracy. There are parts of the intellect that we are not able to test well—like creativity, curiosity, a sense of adventure, ambition. Most of all, America has a culture of learning that challenges conventional wisdom, even if it means challenging authority. These are the areas where Singapore must learn from America. (p. 37)

A culture can be a generation away from losing what it prizes in education. The country that inspired Thomas Edison to give birth to electrical power, recorded music, and motion pictures was dedicated to innovation and imagination. Walsh (2010) notes that Edison's "immense gifts were nurtured by the society in which he flourished, one that reveled in the romance of scientific discovery" (p. 42). While no one can re-create a previous culture in U.S. history, we can pay attention to the educational values that we prize and to how our children learn in this century.

Human beings are complex and learn through complexity. To reduce learning to an input/output construct is to perceive learners as computers to be programmed. The intense focus on testing and AYP has devalued the learner as a human being. Global citizens of the 21st century do indeed need new skills for intellectual survival. If the approach is to simply list the knowledge, skills, and dispositions that we need and then to cover them, we are being short-sighted. We must focus on the unique being who is the learner. We turn to three brief explanations of how humans learn by regarding the work of Jean Piaget, Lev Vygotsky, and brain-based learning theorists.

The Learner: Piaget and Vygotsky

How human beings learn can be explained through three large bodies of work in educational psychology: behaviorism, developmentalism, and cognitivism. While the productivity of behaviorism is compelling, especially teachers' use of reinforcement theory with modeling and thoughtful praise, we emphasize the developmental and cognitive theories of learning. Here are three reasons we do this:

• The learning sciences are expanding cognitive/development theory and practice in exciting ways. This new interdisciplinary field investigates teaching and learning through education, cognitive science, educational psychology, computer science, anthropology, sociology, information sciences, neurosciences, design studies, and instructional design. The overall goal is to reform schools by designing new learning environments to enable deeper, more effective learning (Sawyer, 2006).

• Both developmental and cognitive psychology connect to uniquely human traits of controlling the environment. Behaviorism suggests that living beings respond to stimuli in their environments, rather than shaping them. The cognitivists perceive students as physically *and* mentally active in the classroom (Ormrod, 2004).

• Piaget and Vygotsky are meaning makers for teachers, and their theories fit within the developmental and cognitive realms. The learner is not at the mercy of a manipulated environment but is an entity worthy of self-respect and the respect of the teacher.

The work of Swiss biologist and epistemologist Jean Piaget is still popular because it is the most global theory of intellectual development (Ormrod, 2004). Piagetian theory is relevant to transformational teaching and learning. The Piagetian stages of cognitive development, each with its own unique patterns of thought, are the best-known elements of his psychological theories. Piaget also established *constructivism,* the notion that new ideas and ways of thinking emerge from old ones (diSessa, 2006). Humans learn by building meaning upon prior experiences. Although some research (Siegler, 1998) suggests Piaget may have underestimated children's cognition and overestimated adolescents' or adults' cognitive sophistication, Piaget's learning theories remain.

Piaget found that learning ability develops in an orderly, albeit uneven, fashion. His explanation of how we learn, his learning theory, has often been overlooked. This is unfortunate because it causes us to miss the optimism of his findings and writings about learning. Though maturation of the central nervous system controls the rate of cognitive development to some extent, there is so much more to his theory! Teachers can intervene in the learning environment and make a difference. Some parts of his learning theory can be put into teaching practice:

People are active processors of information. This concept is perhaps the most critical one for teachers to embrace. Unlike his behaviorist contemporaries, Piaget portrayed human beings as individually engaged in interpreting and learning from people and from the physical environment, from others and objects. Thus, for Piaget, the learner is in the center of the learning model. For him the model includes cognitive as well as social goals.

 Others and Objects

A rich classroom learning environment enables students to interact with teachers, peers, and others as well as explore with all the senses our physical, three-dimensional world of objects. The indiscriminate use of worksheets is perhaps the most counter-Piagetian practice in U.S. education. Visitors to worksheet-focused classrooms notice that when they walk through the door, most of the children's heads pop up. In rich learning classrooms, students are so engaged that the visitor becomes a part of the environment almost instantly. In fact, smart teachers have taught their students to use visitors as resources for learning, so visitors may well be asked questions.

Knowledge is stored in a "schema," a mental unit that can change with development. This idea is one of the most optimistic in all of learning theory: The goal of teaching is to effect change in the learner. All students can learn if we tailor classroom learning to start where learners are. Tailoring learning goes beyond the academic to the social and spiritual, which Vygotsky would call the sociocultural. Though individuals' schemas change with experiences, the processes through which people interact with the learning environment remain constant. These processes, called *assimilation* and *accommodation,* are complementary. Assimilation is ingesting new information fitting it into an existing schema. Accommodation involves changing a schema or constructing a new schema to fit the environment. Processing information, knowledge, and experiences is what we call learning. Learning results from a combination of the two processes.

Challenge and Enthusiasm

A teacher shares with her students, "I just saw on the Discovery channel an interesting program relating to our discussion of engineering in ancient Rome." Relating a new experience to what we already know is vital for learning. Stimulating ideas enhanced by teachers' enthusiasm can challenge existing schemata for learners, prompting accommodation to occur. The most vibrant learning takes place in classrooms where teachers are excited about ideas in their subject area and communicate that enthusiasm to their students. The teacher-scholar role is evident here.

Learners are intrinsically motivated to try to make sense of the world. A state of equilibrium is the zone of comfort for a learner to explain new events in terms of existing schemata. Inexplicable or confounding events or information can cause disequilibrium, a mental discomfort sometimes called cognitive dissonance. The movement back and forth between mental comfort and discomfort enables increasingly complex levels of thought and knowledge. Jerome Bruner (1974) explains this process in learners in his discussion of learning modes: (1) concrete or three-dimensional representations of the social and physical world, (2) iconic or pictorial visuals, and (3) symbolic or abstract/theoretical ideas.

Making Abstract Concepts Concrete

The symbolic should be the goal for teachers, but it is not the starting point for most learners. For example, the numeral 23 is an abstract concept until it is explained concretely with base-10 blocks (two 10's and three 1's) or pictorially with an illustration on a page or screen. The concept of place value (usually taught in 2nd grade) is one of the most dissonance-creating concepts learners can encounter in school. In a *Peanuts* cartoon, Snoopy and Woodstock were at a chessboard. Woodstock has a question mark drawn over his head. The cartoon related that playing chess with a checkers mentality is difficult. Teachers must provide scaffolded learning opportunities for students so they can develop new schemata to organize and learn new concepts.

Vygotsky's Theory as Transformational

Another cognitive theorist, Lev Vygotsky (1978), developed the zone of proximal development, a bandwidth of competence that learners use within a supportive context. On one end is an individual's actual developmental level, a comfortable learning level where he can operate with mental independence. At the opposite end is the level of potential development, in which the thinker needs the help of a more sophisticated thinker to understand concepts. Perhaps this sophisticated learner is the teacher. The teacher is the primary force in closing the gap (Shayer & Adey, 2002). To find out where the learner is situated along this bandwidth or continuum, teachers use trial and error. When the instruction matches students' levels, learning occurs more quickly.

A second aspect of Vygotsky's theory is that learning has a social and a spiritual quality where the learner interacts and internalizes ideas. In contrast to Piaget's developmental stages, the Russian psychologist portrayed growth as more seamless and gave greater weight to social context as a stimulator. Children's abilities change through social interaction provided by more capable peers and adults. Teaching methods that prize social interaction or goal structures that encourage cooperative learning are obvious applications of sociocultural learning theory. In the next chapter we will explore guided inquiry teaching, a pedagogical approach rich with sociocultural implications. Vygotsky saw the teacher-student dynamic as having greater potential for cognitive change in the learner, but perhaps this potential is even more expansive.

The relationship found in the teacher-student dynamic is the basis for social constructivist theory, which includes sociocultural belief in transformational learning. The belief has spiritual dimensions if the teacher allows for a relationship of commitment, trust, and respect. The dynamic between teacher and learner is a covenant where the classroom environment is tuned to the potential of the whole child and where students and teachers can embrace the joy of learning.

Socialization can have deeper meaning if teachers commit to a holistic transformation of learners by prizing them as the capable and special beings they are. As Price (2006) states it, "Classroom social systems are organic structures and processes rooted and grounded in an 'invisible/unspoken' sphere of influence and personal power initiated by the classroom teacher" (p. 127). Classrooms are social systems where teachers have enormous personal influence upon students' levels of confidence.

 Vygotsky and Transformational Teaching

Vygotsky's learning concepts demand all three of the teacher-transformer roles of scholar, practitioner, and relater. Teachers who intentionally encourage their students with reflective questions, help them analyze concepts into smaller ideas and tasks, demonstrate how real things work, use formative feedback, and help students meet challenges are helping to close the gap between actual and potential development. Most of us would admit that we routinely seek the easiest or smoothest path in learning and in life. But, with experience, we would also confess that challenges are what promote our growth. So it is with Vygotsky's theory: The best teachers intentionally challenge students in an environment of support.

Alexander (2006) characterizes Vygotsky's direction of development as socialization-to-internalization, in contrast to Piaget's internalization-to-socialization, meaning that Vygotsky emphasized the effects of socialization more than Piaget. Although not as comprehensive a theorist as Piaget, Vygotsky added important social and cultural understandings to developmental theory.

The Learner: Brain-Based Learning Theory

Piaget's and Vygotsky's conceptions of how people learn coincide closely with recent findings in neuroscience. Knowledge of these findings forms an extremely useful foundation for the work of the teacher-practitioner. The brain learns from one neuron communicating with another, forming communities or columns of neurons around significant concepts. Such brain cell chatter cannot occur smoothly until a body of experiences has been developed. Neurons communicate with one another across synapses when stimulated by our sensory experiences. The brain seems to learn best when the following factors can be found in the learning environment:

Challenge: A discrepancy is placed before the learner that is, at least in some respect, outside the mind's understanding or experience.

Novelty: Something new or different stimulates curiosity.

Meaning: The brain perceives the knowledge as having coherence.

Feedback: The learner must have immediate reinforcement of new knowledge.

Repetition: Memory is influenced strongly by repetition of experiences.

Emotion: Knowledge with emotional importance will be remembered.

The teacher's role as a sensitive practitioner is critical in the dimension of challenging students with appropriate curriculum. Challenge to one learner can be frustration or threat to another, and it takes sensitive teachers who are attuned to their students to perceive the difference. Patricia Cranton (2002) writes of an environment of challenge in transformative learning that strikes a balance between support and challenge. Students with lower levels of anxiety can be expected to perform more effectively; correspondingly, frustration leads to overstress, which ultimately blocks or interferes with learning (Eysenck, 1992; Stipek, 1993). A vital understanding (Schunk, 2008; Treffinger & Isaksen, 2005) is that challenge is integral to problem solving in order for learners to generate new ideas.

The brain seems to crave novelty. But when the brain is learning, new information must connect to old. New sensory data are critical to the stimulation of new learning (Schunk, 2008). Other studies of animals show changes in the brain through learning. Rats that were exposed to new opportunities for learning and in a social context with other rats demonstrated an altered cerebral cortex. The combination of others and objects resulted in better performances in rats (Rosenzweig & Bennett, 1978).

So what about studies of human learning? People who have learned to read and write have thicker fibers in their corpus callosums

(Castro-Caldas et al., 1999). And people who learn to play a musical instrument show different organizational patterns in the brain than nonmusicians (Elbert, Pantev, Wienbruch, Rockstroh, & Taub, 1995). The term *plasticity* is used to describe the brain's adaptability to new and different circumstances and experiences.

 Plasticity

Plasticity in the brain is a concept of tremendous optimism for learners if we think about the continuing debate of nature versus nurture. Teachers who complain that they can only do so much with what they have been given can reflect upon the power of plasticity in education. The human brain adapts and changes as it is presented with new and challenging experiences. There are no limitations to what teachers can do in providing nurturing experiences for students. Only our attitudes can hold us back.

Varieties of new data alone are not enough. The learner must perceive meaning or relevancy in the new information in order for it to be stored in the long-term memory. Memory formation takes time for consolidation, where the hippocampus plays a key role (Schunk, 2008). Nonsense data or information perceived to be unrelated to the learner's experience is resisted or rejected by the brain. Ormrod (2004) concludes from synthesis of her research that "meaningful learning promotes better transfer than rote learning" (p. 367), an important insight that should challenge some contemporary classroom practices. This research underlines how important a role teachers play in placing their subject in a meaningful context.

Indeed, the combination of novelty and meaning seems to be at the crux of cognitive process itself. Learning is the interaction between persons and situations—cognitive process is not just what goes on in our minds (Cobb & Bowers, 1999; Schunk, 2008). Students need teachers who continually provide new, meaningful experiences.

 Thematic Units

Trudy teaches 3rd grade in an urban school in Ohio. She looks forward to taking her students to a nearby apple orchard and farm. Her thematic unit integrates several disciplines of study as her class studies where apples are grown (geography); how they are grown and harvested (agriculture, science); what products are made from apples (economics, transportation); and how to measure, graph, and store them (mathematics). Additionally, Trudy's learners paint pictures of the rural landscape (art), sing about Johnny Appleseed (music, history), and write stories (language arts) about apples and their benefits to people. The whole experience is new and meaningful to her students, as they pick apples, run through the trees, observe apple presses, and drink homemade apple cider. Trudy acknowledges that it is a lot of work for her and her school, but it is an indispensable, touchstone learning event for her students every year.

Teachers also play a critical role in the area of feedback. Studies confirm that human beings need reinforcement, especially timely reinforcement, for maximum learning to occur. It is not enough for the learner to encounter meaningful, new information in a challenging context. Nature's stamp of approval, timely feedback, is necessary for the information to transform into knowledge. Feedback can be from humans or inanimate objects such as computers. Simply telling students that their answer is right or wrong (without explanation) has a negative effect on achievement (Marzano et al., 2001). After analyzing almost 8,000 studies on the effects of feedback on achievement, Hattie (1992) concluded, "The most powerful single modification that enhances achievement is feedback. The simplest prescription for improving education must be 'dollops of feedback'" (p. 9). We learn by being corrected by caring teachers.

The fifth factor in brain learning is similar to feedback at least in terms of the value of reinforcing elements in the learning environment. Repetition of individual experience, sometimes called rehearsal by educational psychologists, is a key to memory and learning (Gordon, 2006). Memory can be seen as the "displacement of knowledge a little bit into the future" (p. 1). Neurons must acquire the potential for being able to fire, and their sensitivity is tied to how often they have fired before. Old-fashioned practice after the initial introduction of a concept is part of good teaching, but it must include relevancy, not just rote repetition. Deliberate practice, which takes into account learner characteristics, seems to be a key factor (Schunk, 2008; Singley & Anderson, 1989). This can mean that some students need more repetition than others. Unfortunately, we are quick to label them as slow learners. We often miss the most glaring variable: Students are novice learners to varying degrees and simply lack experience.

The final vital factor in learning is for some the most unlikely: emotion. Our brains are hardwired with the emotions of fear, joy, anger, and sorrow. The amygdala is a small structure located inside and below the brain cortex, deep in the center of the brain. It works extensively with the negative emotions, and it helps us associate particular emotions like fear and anger with particular memories (Adolphs & Damasion, 2001; Byrnes, 2001; Cahill et al., 1996). In fact, it has been suggested that the brain's hippocampus tells us who someone is while the amygdala tells us whether we like them or not.

Though the importance of emotions in education is underestimated, it is not new. Aristotle valued the stimulation of change in knowledge by touching the learner's mind, emotions, and attitude. Recent researchers (Alexander, 2006; Sinatra & Pintrich, 2003) no longer discount emotional influences on motivation and change. The emotional nature of a memory may assist us in our ability to retrieve it—highly intense emotional content is more easily recalled (Reisberg, 1997). Indeed, Ormrod (2004) and Schunk (2008) write that when information is heavy with emotion, it directs our attention and helps us concentrate and elaborate on it over a period of time. The subjective and personal can provide the context and relevance needed for learning (Bredo, 2006; Simpson, 2002).

Rachael Kessler (2000) recommends that teachers "invite joy into their classrooms" (p. 76). Emotion is a key that unlocks learning in the brain. By employing humor, celebrations, physical movement, and enjoyment of nature, teachers will note three positive results: (1) Learners will for a few ecstatic moments move away from their egos and self-absorption; (2) they will see their teachers in a new light, respecting them as real people who share the same emotions as their students; and (3) students will remember what was taught. An inspirational movie, a nature walk, or a simple classroom celebration of a completed assignment can trigger sensations of joy that nurture the human mind and spirit.

Emotions and Spirituality

Consider the learning power of a good story—it always has an emotional element. It explains why we remember certain movies so easily. Great teachers tap into this flow, this synergy of emotion and cognition. Contrary to what many educators have been led to believe, emotion—when used with intentionality and judiciousness—facilitates learning. Emotions are a vital part of who we are. To suggest that a spiritual element in our learning is irrelevant as a goal seems to ignore the role emotions and feelings play in our lives.

Recalling the six brain-based elements of learning is easier with a sentence-mnemonic device. If we scramble the order of the six brain-based facets to **R**epetition, **C**hallenge, **N**ovelty, **M**eaning, **F**eedback, and **E**motion, we can remember them by *Resilient Children Need More Fun Every day.* These elements of brain learning are a vital part of knowing how our students learn. Learning is as complex as the brain, but it is also as profoundly simple as a transformational teacher who knows, does, and cares. Teachers must be scholarly in their subject but also in pedagogy. Thus, knowing and doing unite the scholar and practitioner.

Many approaches to teaching look equivalent when the only dimension and measure of learning is coverage of content and testing for retention. Differences between approaches become apparent when they are evaluated to determine how well learning transfers to new problems and settings (Bransford et al., 2000; Sawyer, 2006). Applying knowledge to new problems and settings is a requirement in the 21st century. Informational teaching cannot serve the needs of modern students and should be abandoned. Transformational teachers equip their students with skills to apply knowledge to new situations and to seek new experiences as lifelong learners.

Final Thoughts

The essential concepts in this chapter focus on the nature of learning. Teachers must know how people learn and be able to apply that knowledge to the learning environment. Many teachers are concerned that the digital culture has changed the way students learn at the expense of literacy and cultural awareness. The most significant theories relating to how human beings learn belong to cognitivists like Piaget, Vygotsky, and brain-based learning researchers. Teachers must understand how learning occurs and especially how to create ideal learning environments where transformation can occur within students.

7

TEACH STUDENTS HOW TO LEARN

The principal goal of education in the schools should be creating men and women who are capable of doing new things, not simply repeating what other generations have done.

Jean Piaget

We must teach so that our students know how to learn. Unknown problems await the inhabitants of the future to a degree that seems unprecedented. The Transformational Pedagogy Model is powerful in its synergy of the intellectual and the spiritual. Why is it so important to use the model? Wondrously accessible information requires the context of an inspiring pedagogical relationship that can encourage students to be independent, responsible learners for life.

The clock metaphor discussed in the introduction implies that informational teaching will not succeed. We simply cannot keep up with the flow of information. Memorization, recitation, and exposition are traditional practices used to demonstrate learning. Such catechetical methodology took its name from religious catechism practices. The ability to memorize and regurgitate became synonymous with learning itself, much like test scores of today have morphed into learning. The modern difference is that students may no longer recite; they display their knowledge on standardized tests.

Today, educators try to cover the waterfront. McTighe, Seif, and Wiggins (2004) contend that, in practice, standards-based teaching can produce overly ambitious lists of essentials for the content areas, adding to the "coverage problem." When we add the propensity of many teachers to focus on textbook teaching, we have further complicated the problem. The competitive ethos calls for an informational teaching mode: By emphasizing breadth and giving their students lots of information, teachers believe they are succeeding. But there is simply not enough time to teach all the standards and benchmarks effectively.

So, what matters most? Deborah Meier (2009) is passionate about teaching the values of democracy, especially when it comes to teaching students to become more independent thinkers, valuing alternative ideas, and being allowed to make choices within the curriculum: "We need to scour the school day for choices that ought to belong to the learner, not just to the teacher, not just to the principal, school board, or state authorities" (pp. 46–47). Choices in classroom learning are vital, but must be tied to student accountability. Assessment is one area in which a transformational teacher can offer students choices.

Rick Stiggins (2007) and Lori Wingo (2009) perceive that informational schooling is losing the concept of individual student accountability in the current educational climate. Schools and teachers are asked to accept the blame for students' lack of proficiency instead of focusing the responsibility on the students. "There are no consequences for the student who takes the test with grudging indifference" (Wingo, p. 1). Teachers and students are partners in the assessment of learning. As Stiggins says:

> When we use assessment for learning, assessment becomes far more than merely a one-time event stuck onto the end of an instructional unit. It becomes a series of interlaced experiences that enhance the learning process by keeping students confident and focused on their progress, even in the face of occasional setbacks. (p. 23)

Schmoker (2009) writes of schools measuring what matters to them, citing an unpleasant discovery as he considers the importance of authentic intellectual tasks and assessments: "Schools and even whole states could make steady gains on standardized tests without offering students intellectually challenging tasks" (p. 71). Test-prep activities are responsible for much of the increase in achievement scores. Ironically, as Schmoker notes, testing data itself seems to be creating a ceiling on instructional improvement.

 Educational Issues

U.S. education seems to be at a watershed moment. Transformational teaching as a concept can assist. As we worry about teaching the basics in our schools, we tend to deprioritize socialization and omit enriching ideas that come from student inquiry. Let's summarize the educational issues:

- Diverse student populations are posing new challenges for teachers.
- Traditional schooling is not working.
- New technologies and media compete for learners' attention.
- Accountability and standards-based teaching leave little room for pedagogical flexibility, and teachers as relaters are devalued.
- The product of improved test scores has obliterated the process of learning, the joy of discovering, and the power of individual research.
- Conventional schooling cannot be repaired with punitive laws and rigid policies because they destroy teachers' creativity and students' motivation and curiosity.

Trusting the Process

What does the Transformational Pedagogy Model contribute toward confronting educational issues? Why use the model instead of other current practices? Using the model provides inclusion of two vital concepts in teaching and learning often missing in this era: inspiration and strategic learning qualities. The focus on relationships can inspire an illuminating best in holistic education, including core human spiritual values like trust, responsibility, and resilience. Strategic learning qualities encourage a focus on the students that is supported by the importance of deep understanding and lifelong learning. Process skills come from learners engaged in asking questions under the guidance of a teacher. Teachers who teach for inspiration and for process will *engage* their students. Strategic learning qualities are timeless skills of cognition, motivation, and personal responsibility.

Engaging students holistically requires that our learners truly be in the center of education. Bob Sullo (2007) relates a story about Ben, a middle school counselor, who realizes that students were not leaving his school with a greater love of learning or appreciation for the value of a good education. His behaviorist orientation worked only with compliant kids whose locus of control was external. They worked to be rewarded for minimally competent work or to avoid retention or summer school. Once Ben began to view his role from the perspective of internal motivation, he began to see himself as a successful counselor-relater who helped students become good decision makers. Good teaching, like good counseling, seems to require a greater appreciation of the relationship between educator and learner. Ben moved to a more cognitive perspective, a more long-term, process-oriented paradigm. Engaging students requires that teachers relinquish some power, allowing students to accept responsibility for their own work as well as their own identities.

Using Strategic Learning Qualities

The strategic learning qualities introduced in Chapter 3 include openness, skepticism, civility, persistence, imagination, and curiosity. These qualities promote deep understanding and exemplify intellectual processing that stands in contrast to the more product-oriented emphasis of the Information Age. Strategic learning qualities are process instruments used to achieve deep understanding and a love of lifelong learning.

Students who know how to learn, use strategic learning qualities effectively. We must expect more from our schooling, hold onto what is of value from the past, and use new tools of learning in the future. If deep knowledge and knowing how to learn is the destination, these learner qualities are the road less taken. Students acquire strategic learning qualities from the following pedagogical experiences:

- Immersion in pedagogy that allows teacher and learners to make choices about what is learned. The knowledge explosion in our world guarantees that teaching for coverage is fruitless.

- Teachers who demand more from students. Great pedagogy encompasses comprehensiveness and authenticity. Pedagogy can be comprehensive when it guards against the tunnel vision of the latest trends. It is authentic when it mirrors real-world problems and questions in modern intellectual structures that dig beneath some of the shallowness of the digital age.

- Intellectual challenges that are buttressed with nurturing teachers. Students reach their learning potential when social supports are present in the learning environment. Coupling intellectual challenge with social support creates a dynamic set of pedagogical factors that engages learners.

- Teachers who know and remember that they have not taught anything until someone has learned it.

- Teachers who engage students' curiosity and believe that curiosity is a universal human learning trait. Connecting to curiosity is a spiritual goal of education. Innate curiosity should not be taken for granted. The institution of school seems to have a way of blunting or dismantling it. Teachers of secondary students often despair that the trait even exists.

 Learning Success Is the Measure of Teaching Success

Consider this old homily: "I taught my dog Fluffy to whistle." A second person asks, "Why then is he not whistling?" And the reply is "Because he didn't learn it." Teachers are often labeled as good or great because they are charismatic and spellbinding as lecturers. If we peel off the veneer of this labeling practice, we often find that these same teachers reach the "good to great" students only. These teachers fail to connect to the experience and motivation levels of the "bad students." One striking piece of folk pedagogy is the tendency both from inside and outside the education profession to misjudge what good teaching really is.

If evidence suggests that learning is not occurring, we need to slow down and inspect the total learning environment, including the goal structures, the curriculum, the teachers, the students, and our pedagogies. We must develop a plan for improving the learning environment to engage students for success.

Active and Engaged Learning

A plan for engaging students should include attention to active learning. The term itself perhaps implies more than is there. Teachers may wonder if they have been promoting passive learning. As brain research supports, there is no such thing as passive learning. Our brains are too sophisticated and complex to accept such a notion. Teachers who promote active learning create a learning environment that fosters growth. The ideal learning environment is academically, socially, and spiritually holistic. The best way to create this environment is to connect to students' individual experiences, challenge them with good questions and problems, and provide timely feedback on their learning.

The term *engaged* as compared to *active* is preferred by many learner-centered educators because it connotes connection. Transformational teachers connect to their students as practitioners and relaters of their discipline. McCombs and Miller (2006) say, "When learners are being effortful and strategic during learning, they are engaged and learning to optimal levels" (p. 55).

 Engaged Learning

Brain scientists and many cognitivists agree on at least two aspects of learning: (1) learning occurs when a connection is made to prior experiences (Shulman, 1999); and (2) within the brain itself, learning connections are made between neurons when meaningful data are involved (Greenough, Black, & Volkmar, 1979; Ormrod, 2004). The term *engaged* is meant to connote a classroom dynamic where the student and the teacher are coupled together in the same intellectual and socioemotional construct. In terms of education, they are engaged, or intellectually and socially connected. Engaged learning goes beyond active learning to connection to prior experiences.

....

Learning that occurs from memorizing, listening, reciting, and quizzing is what Beyer (1971) famously called "lesson hearing." The teacher is more active intellectually and physically than the learner, who is cast in the sponge-like passive role. Such pedagogy is useful and efficient for covering subject matter, but the teacher is doing most of the work. Robyn Jackson (2009) asserts that teachers underestimate student abilities and overestimate teacher contributions. She elevates this concept to a pedagogical principle: Never work harder than your students! For our students to know how to learn, they must be not just allowed to but also encouraged to learn more independently.

These ideas are based on a cognitive psychology that presumes all students possess a genuine interest and an innate curiosity for discovering new ideas and seeking solutions to relevant problems. Pedagogy that reveals this often deeply buried quality in learners will be successful (Bransford et al., 2000; Ormrod, 2004). Pedagogy that includes active techniques of inquiry matches purposes of discovery better than the traditional pedagogy of exposition.

Discovery and Inquiry Teaching

Jerome Bruner deserves credit for pioneering the popularity of discovery learning pedagogy upon which inquiry teaching is based. His theory states that students learn best when they use what they know as the basis for new learning, as contrasted with merely telling learners what we as teachers believe they need to know (Alexander, 2006). The demands on learners of this century and an emergent understanding of how humans learn move us toward recovery of and reacquaintance with teaching and learning through inquiry.

Inquiry teaching is closely related to discovery learning, problem-based learning, project-approach learning, experiential learning, and constructivist learning (Helm, 2004; Kirschner, Sweller, & Clark, 2006). We will define it in its methodology as guided, scientific inquiry. The teacher directs and arranges the learning environment according to a pre-planned question or problem. The students learn by questioning, exploring, gathering, and synthesizing information under the guidance of the teacher.

Authentic Learning

Blumenfeld, Kempler, and Krajcik (2006) argue that cognitive engagement can be attained through an inquiry approach that motivates by "influencing value and perceived autonomy" (p. 480). Feelings of value for students come from authentic learning, from tying classroom activities to real-world topics and academic disciplines. For example, a chemistry colleague connected the academic classroom to authentic learning by studying coffee beans at a local Starbucks. Students analyzed bean acidity, growing conditions, roasting effect, grind, and brewing influences. They displayed their findings on posters at the Starbucks store.

A sense of autonomy for students emerges from the process of collecting, analyzing, and interpreting information. Despite the complexity of modern life, such engagement can be initiated by a simple but well-considered question. The power of the question can be dynamically fused with the wonder of the digital age. Guided inquiry—asking questions—provides the opportunity for students to interact with digital media in a productive, research-oriented fashion. The process of guided inquiry also highlights the role of social interaction in learning, where teachers, students, and community members work together in authentic settings to construct shared understanding (Krajcik & Blumenfeld, 2006).

Guided Inquiry Teaching

To engage students, teachers need pedagogy that competes with digital toys, omnipresent media, shorter attention spans, and shifts in value systems. Digital toys and media can be allies for learning, but only if the teacher-practitioner employs reflective pedagogy that meets learners on their own turf. Many students have embraced learning using web-based instruction and interactive and self-paced technologies inside and outside school. The supply of online resources is staggering. Teachers can take advantage of numerous online resources by structuring individual and group learning through inquiry. Inquiry learning can combine new digital technology with the classic power of questions.

Shorter attention spans and shifts in value systems can be addressed by an academically rigorous teacher-relater. Sam Intrator (2004) suggests "anti-boredom pedagogy" like going outside for class, introducing dramatic footage from a video, bringing visitors into the classroom, or dressing up in costume. The key element in guided inquiry is good questions that tie everything together. Reflective teaching can address the needs, fears, and interests of young students. Reflective teachers find that student questions often reveal that students attempt to use the learning context to find out who they are—part of identifying their value systems. And enthusiastic and expressive teachers who listen to their students breed authentic, holistic, and engaged learners.

The Internet is changing the way we inquire in school. Scardamalia and Bereiter (2006) write about a shift from treating students as individual inquirers to treating them as members of a knowledge-building community. They envision the Internet as "more than a desktop library and a rapid mail-delivery system. The Internet is a realistic means for students to connect with civilization-wide knowledge building and to make their classroom work part of it" (p. 98).

 Bruner's Guided Inquiry

During the 1960s, Jerome Bruner led efforts in the social and natural sciences as well as in mathematics to encourage learning by discovery, guided discovery, and inquiry learning. The simple pedagogical idea is still effective: Allow students to work at creating their own learning, and they will remember what they learn. Teacher-directed or guided inquiry occurs when the teacher directs and plans in-depth exploration by the students. It is similar to project-based pedagogy, which tends to be more student initiated in form. The label should not be a barrier to understanding the power of inquiry for deep understanding. Every guided inquiry lesson should result in an individual or group exhibition or project. Research has demonstrated that learners in project-based classrooms achieve more than students in traditional classrooms (Marx et al., 2004; Rivet & Krajcik, 2004).

Inquiry teaching is not a panacea or the solution to how we can teach. To think that pedagogy could consist of just one approach to teaching and learning is misguided and mistaken both in theory and practice. But we have chosen guided inquiry teaching as a source of hope because it holds the best potential for transformational pedagogy that can both inspire and teach students to be lifelong learners. Teaching for inquiry learning is a broad-based approach to student learning that subsumes many approaches, like project-based pedagogy.

Inquiry learning is active, cross-disciplinary, problems based, cooperative, and flexible. Inquiry learning must be intentional. Indeed, the emerging field of learning sciences increasingly reinforces the value of intentional learning across disciplines through problem solving. Researchers have found that practicing problem solving leads learners to develop cognition sets that are less likely to limit their flexibility in solving new problems, and that cooperative groups often facilitate problem solving (Carr & Biddlecomb, 1998; Chen, 1999). Problem solving is an integral part of inquiry teaching. Schunk (2008) helps us define it:

> The problem may be to answer a question, compute a solution, locate an object, secure a job, teach a student, and so on. *Problem solving* refers to people's efforts to achieve a goal for which they do not have an automatic solution. (p. 196)

Clearly the concept of problem solving involves a certain dissonance for the learner, a disruption of the equilibrium so that the solution is not automatic. Such dissonance is necessary for learning; indeed, it is the foundation of Piaget's (1969) idea of cognitive growth.

 Context and Process

The context of inquiry teaching and learning is important. Educators must not lose track of what is to be learned and why. Bruner (1974) warned "Discovery was being treated by some educators as if it were valuable in and of itself, no matter what it was a discovery of or in whose service" (p. 15). Here again is our either/or tendency: We must avoid falling in love with the process of inquiry and forgetting the product, knowledge. Inquiry teaching establishes real problems that require searching for background knowledge, teacher modeling of good questions, and continual feedback. The process patiently poses questions or issues, explores possibilities, and seeks resolutions.

Inquiry as Pedagogy

Inquiry plays a strong role in science and the social studies, but it can be applied to all disciplines because it uses the scientific method of discovery. Here are the fundamental ideas of guided inquiry:

• Relies upon the profound power of questions—always the teacher's best tool—from both the teacher and the students.

• Places teachers in a facilitator role that orchestrates inquiry discussion and assessment. This role reduces exposition, but it also makes the teacher a stronger arbitrator of knowledge with a focus on formative assessment.

• Gives the teacher a provider role that includes preparing a good problem to solve and preparing resources for the students to use. It is very important that learners do not become so initially frustrated in finding solutions that they capitulate in their learning. Questions must represent problems that are moderate in challenge—that fit the experience level of the learners.

• Encourages natural curiosity in intermediate grades through higher education, which is precisely when it is needed because of the tendency of traditional schooling to discourage asking of questions as learners move through the grade levels.

• Places learners in an active discovery role and asks students to seek their own information and create their own knowledge. The discovery role allows for the needed temporary experiences of failure that trial-and-error learning can produce.

• Stresses process skills in learning. Inquiry is complex in that it requires process skills as well as literacy and numeracy skills. Process skills include strategic learning qualities as well as the ability to ask relevant questions, to conduct searches on the Internet and in libraries, and to work with other students in a coherent, organized manner with direction from the teacher.

Inquiry teaching is a pedagogy designed to be more student directed than traditional approaches that employ teacher direction or didacticism. Inquiry teaching is an approach that fits our digital age. Figure 7.1 demonstrates the opposite nature of inquiry and didactic pedagogies.

FIGURE 7.1
Pedagogical Continuum

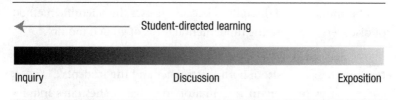

The continuum can be misleading if we jump to certain conclusions or assumptions such as pedagogy on the left and middle is good—anything on the right is bad. Or, we could assume that exposition necessarily excludes discussion and inquiry. Or, vice versa, that inquiry necessarily excludes lecture or discussion as pedagogical choice. How we teach must fit the teacher, the curriculum, and the student; and methods can—and often should—vary, even within a single lesson. Every teaching technique has assets and liabilities. The pedagogy continuum is only useful if we keep in mind that it is indeed a continuum that expresses degrees of student-directed or teacher-directed learning. Exposition tends to be teacher directed in definition and function. Its purpose is usually for highlighting for students what teachers think is important.

The pedagogical continuum has more subtle applications.

Active learning is an instructional perspective that can be found on many points of the continuum, as it can encompass a wide range of teaching strategies. It always engages the learner in the instruction taking place (Orlich et al., 2007). Thus, traditional lecture, if it is done well and takes into account learners' attention spans, can inspire active learning.

Inquiry teaching is clearly defined by student-directed pedagogy. It is based on intellectual confrontations and has the goal of independent learning. When students explore concepts independently, their minds are more likely to be engaged.

Engaged learning can occur all along the continuum, from inquiry to expository teaching. Logically, however, engagement occurs more consistently when students direct their own learning. As we said earlier, we have not taught until our students learn. Guided inquiry teaching connects to the way learning occurs.

Engaged learning occurs when the teaching is meaningful to students. Good questions drive good inquiry. To further ensure interest for the students and value for the community, Krajcik and Blumenfeld (2006) recommend that teachers align "driving questions" with standards like the following one from the National Science Education Standards: "A substance has characteristic properties, such as density, a boiling point, and solubility, all of which are independent of the amount of the sample" (1996 Content Standard B5-8: 1A). The authors describe their process of meeting with teachers and discussing possible driving questions (those questions that create relevance and interest for students):

> Some seemed too trivial and did not lead to opportunities for students to explore phenomena. We finally settled on "How do I make new stuff from old stuff?" and we created an anchoring experience [project] of making soap as an example of making new stuff from old stuff. (p. 323)

Learning sciences research (Blumenfeld et al., 1991; Bransford et al., 2000) shows more effective learning occurs when learners are allowed to interact with artifacts—external representations of knowledge—like physical models, reports, videotapes, drawings, games, and computer models. Judy Helm (2004) describes how young students can interact with the artifact of corn:

> During a project exploring corn at Discovery Preschool, the students were intrigued by the idea that corn could become other things. The project became focused on the question, "What things have corn in them?" The students interviewed an expert from a corn processing plant. Then these 3- and 4-year-olds learned how to find the word *corn* on ingredient labels, and they collected packages of products with corn. One student woke her mother in the middle of the night to fetch the frozen pizza wrapping from the garbage to see whether the pizza had corn in it. Children learned to not only read and write the word *corn* but also write the names of the items they collected. (p. 60)

Not only did students gain understanding of the main topic, corn, but they also made exciting connections to a relevant, real-world body of knowledge. Krajcik and Blumenfeld (2006) give three conditions for effectiveness: artifacts that address driving questions, that show the emerging understanding of learners, and that support students in developing understanding associated with the learning goals of the project. This coincides with Bruner's admonition and research that student-directed learning, like inquiry, needs to be focused, sequential, and carefully tied to what students know. Inquiry learning needs to be guided by the teacher.

Inquiry as the Scientific Method

Inquiry teaching is described as the scientific method employed as pedagogy. Inquiry teaching is applied as critical thinking or discovery learning. Because the scientific process is compressed into smaller windows of time (Joyce & Weil, 2004), the focus is more on the process than the product of learning. In fact, the end product might be relatively unimportant compared to the processes used to create it because the processes involved teaching the use of learning skills. Such skills become the foundation for lifelong learning. Remember Bruner's admonition that we should not forget *what* we are trying to teach. Our goals affect our pedagogy.

Discovery learning has its limits. Research has found that unguided discovery learning is an impediment for inexperienced learners (Tuovinen & Sweller, 1999). Compared with guided instruction (Mayer, 2004), unguided discovery learning is ineffective and limited in its connections to working memory (Kirschner et al., 2006). By contrast, guided inquiry teaching can free learners to think critically as they solve problems involving many kinds of knowledge.

The general model of guided inquiry mirrors the scientific method in its steps: identifying a problem, proposing hypotheses, collecting evidence, interpreting and testing the evidence, drawing tentative conclusions, retesting, and then forming a firm conclusion.

Inquiry teaching does not need to dominate a teacher's peda-gogical approach. Indeed, it is a good idea not to use this pedagogy predominantly. Why? One reason has to do with fit. As we have emphasized, locking into one type of pedagogy is not desirable. Teachers need to use different methods to fit the curriculum and the students, and to fit their teaching styles. Another reason not to become overly enamored with inquiry is that inquiry teaching takes time, often twice as much class time as compared to traditional meth-ods. It takes more time not only because of the interaction between the teacher and learner, but also because of the increased time on topical research, which is usually quite interdisciplinary. The time spent is worth it, however, if deep, meaningful understanding occurs.

Another reason that inquiry should not dominate but comple-ment other approaches is the students themselves. Learners will resist hard work, especially if it seems unreasonable in quantity and narrow in variety. Doyle (2008) says the biggest challenge we face in learner-centered teaching is "getting our students to buy into the change, to switch their learning paradigm" (p. 17). It is a human quality to adopt a comfort zone in learning as well as in life. Our students are used to teacher-directed, even teacher-dominated classrooms.

As cited earlier, Jackson (2009) implores us to switch this para-digm by conceiving of our students as workers, not listeners. Teachers can think of it as teaching through inquiry as opposed to teaching from something. Guided inquiry teaching still teaches toward goals, and the teacher's work is still challenging. But the hardest work in this model is preparing the research questions and projects. Teachers must focus the questions and problems, provide resources and refer-ences, and strategize assessment.

As we change our teaching paradigm to include inquiry teaching, teachers must maintain sensitivity to student needs, with a focus on nurturing relationships and transforming learners. Trusting this pro-cess and respecting the integrity of our learners' desire to learn will allow learning paradigms to change more smoothly. By shifting to a more student-directed learning model with a focus on key questions, we hold our students to a deeper level of accountability.

Final Thoughts

We began this book by focusing on how rapidly our world is changing. How can we teach students today so that they continue to learn
tomorrow and for a lifetime? Teachers can give students a great gift by
teaching them how to learn with inspired, rigorous process-oriented
teaching like guided inquiry. Such teaching connects not only with
learners' innate curiosity but also with new technologies for driving their topical research. In the process students learn to use strategic learning qualities of openness, skepticism, persistence, civility,
imagination, and curiosity. The students' learning is not only active
but engaged academically, socially, and spiritually. We placed guided
inquiry teaching on a pedagogical continuum with exposition and
discussion to highlight the understanding that teaching must fit the
learning circumstances and that teachers should not make snap judg-
ments about good and bad pedagogy. Transformational pedagogy prioritizes teachers' nurturing relationships with students, places them
at the center of the classroom, seeks to connect to their prior experiences, and challenges them with problems to solve.

8

TEACH BY ASKING QUESTIONS

We can't solve problems by using the same kind of thinking we used when we created them.

Albert Einstein

Inquiry teaching is a natural, logical outgrowth of cognitive theory because of its reliance on and trust in a learner's innate curiosity. To inquire is to express a need to know something, even to seek a challenge. The most effective instrument in the teacher's tool box is a good question. We should teach by asking questions. Teachers as experts best exemplify the scholar role by being interrogative rather than declarative.

Students are novice learners as they express their need to know through inquiry learning. To inquire is to ask many questions. By encouraging student questions, teachers can design learning experiences around meaningful problems that entice students to inquire. Neuroscientists tell us that humans seek patterns and order out of confusion and chaos. A good problem, especially when it is expressed as a good question, presents enough cognitive dissonance that the learner is eager to engage his curiosity. We are all curious about how our world works. Brooks (2004) expresses our human need to know as a search for meaning:

> Why a piece of music is beautiful to one person and cacophonous to another, how engines are able to make cars move, why green leaves turn brown and helium balloons stay aloft, or how new languages develop. Living means perpetually searching for meaning. Schools need to be places that keep this search alive. (p. 12)

Transformational teaching takes time. Many years ago, a car oil-filter company ran a television commercial showing a customer who had neglected to change his oil and had to cope with a car engine that had overheated and died. The message of the oil-stained grease monkey was "Pay me now or pay me later." The car will need service, in the form of either preventive maintenance or crisis management. In our schools we seem to believe that taking the time to teach for deep, meaningful understanding on a regular basis is incompatible with meeting standards. We will pay for it later when our students not only do not learn with deep understanding but also are turned off from lifelong learning by the grind of contemporary schooling.

Less with More

McTighe et al. (2004) remind us that teachers can best raise test scores "by teaching in rich and engaging ways" (p. 27). Inquiry teaching can be extremely rich and engaging but takes more time for intentional, detailed planning and for extended student research. The benefits are significant. A regular, short-term academic investment in teaching using inquiry will pay dividends in students' adult lives.

A well-worn phrase that applies to education and life in general is "less is more." According to recent research by Schwartz, Sadler, Sonnert, and Tai (2008), the phrase needs to be modified to "less *with* more." Their longitudinal study tracked 8,310 high school science students to measure their success rates in college science. The study revealed that those students who studied fewer topics with more depth were more positively, significantly affected than those who studied more topics with less depth. Those who spent one month or more studying one major topic in depth in high school earned higher grades in college science than those who studied more topics in the same period of time. In-depth study is essential to education because of how the brain learns by growing dendrites that connect, based on meaning, into networks. In-depth study leads to deeper understanding, leading to development of lifelong learning skills.

 Postholing

The elegant horse farms near Lexington, Kentucky, can inspire transformational teaching. Think about traditional teaching pedagogy being compared with the fencing surrounding the vast tracts of land found on horse farms. Beautiful fencing encircles and encloses the green, rolling land, providing boundaries for the horses. The external boundaries of the farms remind us of teachers covering content material in broad, expansive units and lessons. Consider, though, the fence posts that support the lovely, fence structure. Each posthole was dug by the fence builder, stopping at regular intervals and digging deep into the ground. Students need teachers to stop and "dig in," to allow in-depth analysis of content. Posthole pedagogy provides the support and meaning that are essential for learning.

Teachers who use inquiry reduce the emphasis on the amount of content covered and increase the time spent on content taught through process skills, including problem solving and strategic learning qualities. Guided inquiry is appropriate for all the grades, but teachers must be sensitive to developmental levels of learners. Research (Schmidt, 2004; Schmidt, Houang, & Cogan, 2002) has shown that students in high-achieving countries who were offered fewer topics coupled with more focused content allowed teachers to delve more deeply into subject matter. Such a focus on coherent content and deep understanding is vital and should be seen as part of a balanced approach to pedagogy. In other words, there is a time for the efficiency of exposition and traditional methods, and a time for more student-oriented pedagogy like inquiry with an emphasis on thinking skills.

The most common way of presenting an inquiry lesson is through a question to answer or a problem to solve. The question must connect with the learners' experiences and motivate them to find an answer. Marzano et al. (2001) say that asking students to generate and test hypotheses, which is the essence of inquiry teaching, is one of the most powerful and analytic of cognitive operations. To formulate a hypothesis is also an intuitive mental exercise. We are asking students to make educated guesses; they have the opportunity to respond to questions based on valid evidence. Students use strategic learning qualities by being open, skeptical, imaginative, and curious when they pose a hypothesis. As they solve the problem or answer the question, they display persistence and are led to develop civility in working with others.

The method used to begin a lesson is critical to both motivation and understanding. Beginning with good questions is the best method for engaging students. A principle in educational psychology encourages teachers to cue students into the lesson or activity they are about to teach. David Ausubel called them advance organizers. The thinking is that we should teach content to our students from "whole to part." By advancing students into what we are about to teach, we help them organize their learning. In application, it can be as simple as the teacher saying, "Here are the three things we are going to discuss today." Teachers use cues, or hints, about what is to come in the lesson, such as when teachers tell their students about specific expectations: "Today we will learn about the synergy and tension between democracy and capitalism. Why are these two concepts so important in our lives?"

Shaping Questions is a cue experience that can be used before a film or activity as a cue or afterward as formative assessment. The exercise in Figure 8.1 can be done quickly in writing, and, when done orally, it has never failed to engender discussion.

Good questions can focus learners. Relevancy to the topic piques student interest (Alexander, 2006). Higher-order questions produce deeper learning. When forming a question, we want to carefully build in meaning and depth. Relevance and higher-order questions are the key elements of guided inquiry that allow us to put this useful pedagogical theory into practice.

FIGURE 8.1
Shaping Questions

Using your notes, materials, or memory, please address the following questions.

▪ Look for some things you will hear, see, say, or do that "*square*" with your beliefs. OR,
What are some things you heard, saw, said, or did that "*squared*" with your beliefs?

▲ As you watch and listen, make note of *three* key points to remember. OR,
What are *three* points you wish to remember from our session?

● As you watch and listen, list some questions going *around* in your head. OR,
What are some questions still going *around* in your head?

Guided Inquiry Applications

Applying the theory of guided inquiry requires a relevant topic. Students of U.S. history invariably study the Civil War. Initially, this topic may or may not have meaning for students, depending on how it is taught. Indeed, if the teacher assigns a chapter and asks the students to analyze the causes of the U.S. Civil War, the topic may have little relevance for them. What if, however, the instructor asks, "What was it like to live during the Civil War?" This question opens many possibilities, especially if the teacher follows up with an interesting springboard like an authentic set of letters written by a Southern family in the early 1860s. The letters chronicle the communication between the boys who are serving on the battlefields and their parents at home. The inquiry teaching lesson could go something like this:

1. Beginning

- Ask the question.
- Describe the setting of the South during the Civil War, and distribute the letters for the students to read.

• Ask the students to brainstorm about what they have read, what they found in the letters that was interesting, or what they are curious about.

• Record every response on a whiteboard, encouraging students in their thinking and not allowing fellow students to discourage responses. After a specified amount of time, the teacher analyzes and sorts the responses into categories, such as communication, health, education, the war itself, family cultures, religion—all in the context of the question "What was it like to live during the Civil War?" Note the cross-disciplinary implications of this pedagogy.

2. Investigation

• Divide the class into groups according to the topics, allowing the students to choose their area as much as possible. Each group is assigned a topical research project. The Internet is an excellent source for topical research.

• Students need guidance from teachers during inquiry teaching lessons. Conferences with inquiry research groups are helpful for focusing students' investigations. Teachers may ask a variety of questions: What is your plan for research? Do you have a realistic time frame? How do you plan to exhibit your learning? Teachers can also ask guiding questions to assist students struggling with finding relevant information.

• Emphasize individual responsibility for meaningful contributions to the group work. Through inquiry and presentation of learning, team members develop the vital strategic learning qualities of openness to others and ideas, a clarifying skepticism toward problem solving, a persistence in topical research in overcoming obstacles to "get it right," civility in listening to others, imagination for embracing new approaches, and curiosity to seek resolution.

3. Conclusion

• Each research group exhibits their learning at an appropriate time under set criteria.

• All students are tested on the information presented by all groups.

We can look for at least six important factors in the inquiry lesson:

- A meaningful question provided by the teacher in the context of curriculum goals—the relevance and strength of the question is critical for success
- An interesting springboard
- A "handoff" to the students so that they can articulate their own, more specific questions to answer
- An encouraging process that includes preplanning by the teacher in providing data and readily available resources to enable a smooth initiation of research
- A reasonable deadline and presentation parameters for completion of the project
- A comprehensive assessment "summing up" the formative pieces of the assignment

Guided Inquiry Lessons

Asking good questions relates to teaching strategies. When we phrase a question like "Who was Thomas Edison and what inventions did he create?" we limit the lesson to what the teacher thinks is important for students to know. But, if we ask, "How can we discover who Thomas Edison was and what he did?" we open the lesson to inquiry instead of emphasis on information alone (Welton & Mallan, 1998). Here are just a few guided inquiry lessons that exemplify how the power of good questions can stimulate learning:

Lesson on presidents: Guided inquiry teaching can allow students to probe their own lives even as they study the biography of a U.S. president. The title for this exercise might be "Adams's Monumental Absence," taken from a like-named article in *The Washington Times,* March 14, 2008. Begin the lesson by introducing John Adams, second president of the United States, to the students by asking, "Why do you think no monument has been erected for John Adams in Washington, D.C., since our country's founding in 1776?" Explain that not only was he our second president, but he also was instrumental in the first and second Continental Congresses, helped draft the Declaration of Independence, and otherwise assisted in shaping the philosophical basis for the American Revolution. Next, as a springboard for the inquiry lesson, show over the course of three days the 2008 HBO miniseries "John Adams," which is based on historian David McCullough's 2001 biography. After each program in the series, brainstorm with students by asking shaping questions: What did you see that agrees (squares) with what you already knew about Adams or other founders? Give me three points or ideas (triangle) that you think are important or significant. As a result of your viewing the program, what ideas or thoughts are going around (circling) in your head? Carefully record the students' responses for later use. After the miniseries has been shown, group the students with three research topics/projects based on their brainstorming ideas, like: What were Washington and Jefferson like as real people? What influence did Abigail Adams have on John and the founding years of the United States? What is the history of the funding and building of monuments in our nation's capital? After the reports or projects have been done, reask the question "Why neglect John Adams?" Someone will surely say that Adams was a difficult and cantankerous man, lacking the charisma of Jefferson and other honored Virginians. Then, explore why personalities and relationships are important. Ask students about leadership: "What are the important characteristics of great leaders?" The goal of this lesson is to study the dynamics of the founding of the nation with a focus on the people who were most involved. The goal is also to allow students to ask questions and find answers that will give them insight into their own personalities and experience as U.S. citizens in this century. This guided inquiry lesson will allow students to dig (posthole) into American history, making deep connections that a traditional lesson will not allow. It will require two weeks for completion, and it is designed for upper elementary through high school students.

Lesson on math: Donna Breault (2005) gives a beautiful illustration of a first-year, 5th grade teacher. The young teacher presented a mathematics problem as her primary focus. As is typical of discovery learning, other subjects came into play. Students were given a piece of paper with an outline of a shopping mall with stores of various shapes and sizes. The problem: What is the appropriate monthly rent for the stores in the mall? The only information provided was the rent for one of the stores. No store dimensions were provided. This problem of "the incomplete," which solicits deductive thinking, tapped into the students' experiences and challenged their thinking as they worked in groups.

Lesson on social studies: A classic social studies example is called "Mystery Island" (Zevin, 1969). The teacher asks, "Where would you locate a city?" and then proceeds to provide information in a sequenced series of pictures of an island. Each overlay provides more information: The first one gives basic topography like rivers, bays, and mountains. The second overlay adds temperature and rainfall. The students, divided into competing groups, are asked for an informed opinion after each overlay is put down. The lesson teaches patience, places a premium on the application of geographical knowledge, and culminates with the teacher providing the answer. The exercise moves inductively from the specific sets of data to a general conclusion. The surprise answer is that the mystery island is Australia turned upside down.

 ### Centration and Egocentrism

Each example lesson is fueled by a relevant question that is suited for students from the intermediate grades through college. The guided inquiry lessons are not relevant or appropriate for most primary-age children because they do not have the knowledge and experience to build upon and many would have difficulty with the process itself, especially with civility. A common difficulty for preschoolers is that they may lose sight of the problem as a whole by attending to only one goal at a time. This difficulty fits with the developmental understanding called centration, that young children tend to center on one idea to the exclusion of all else. Another characteristic of young children is egocentrism—they are often unable to perceive others or objects from any point of view other than their own. This concept typically does not involve an attitude of selfishness but instead is a developmental issue.

Judy Helm (2004) writes persuasively of the possibilities for young children inquiring through project-based learning. Her salient point is that following the interests and using the questions of young children, with less teacher direction, can lead them to higher-level thinking. She encourages more spontaneity with preschool students, allowing them to use their experience and unique language expression. The conclusion of such inquiry can range from simply telling a story in a book, to open houses, to documentation like photographs, journals, and portfolios.

As experience and maturity develop, children can learn to work cooperatively and collaboratively. Teachers of young children must give patient guidance with an understanding of their learners' developmental stage. Young children are experts in curiosity and ask great questions that need to be explored. While group work may need to be limited, primary students can still be led to discover wonder by enthusiastic teachers. With adult support, younger children can benefit from more independent, topical research with challenging questions providing stimulus.

Inquiry, Engagement, and the Model

Inquiry teaching can be focused on questions as well as specific problems to solve. Inquiry teaching must be a deliberate event. Instructors must understand the process, be objective, suspend their personal opinions, and be comfortable as facilitators. Inquiry teaching, while applicable to all subject areas, seems best suited for content that requires knowledge beyond the facts. It reaches for the top of Bloom's taxonomy.

 Inquiry Teaching Explores All Disciplines

Situations that involve the implications of social or scientific action or inaction are ideal for the inquiry method. As such, they involve reflection and judgment and often subsume many subject areas. Thus, the problem may be social science in its expression, but if the problem is well formulated, learners will encounter and learn mathematics, natural and physical science, the arts, and other disciplines. Inquiry teaching explores all sides of issues and the effects on humankind. But teachers must make time for wonder. As Jacqueline Brooks (2004) quotes a new teacher, "Our job is to get students to love learning and wonder why and how things work" (p. 12).

Because inquiry teaching builds upon the natural curiosity of individuals, it honors their questions and creates a climate where observations and tentative decisions can flow freely without fear of inappropriate constraints. It creates an environment conducive to the transformation of the learner because lessons are student centered and reflection based. Inquiry teaching mimics the natural questioning of a reflective thinker that may go unexpressed for fear of judgment or ridicule. It is critical that guided discovery learning take place in a risk-free learning environment with a supportive teacher where minds can be engaged.

Pedagogy like guided inquiry teaching that promotes engaged learning is desirable, not as an end in itself but as a means to transformational learning. It can create a learning environment where inspiration and imagination can flourish. Walter Isaacson (2007), in his profound biography of Einstein, reminds us of the great physicist's words: "Imagination is more important than knowledge" (p. 7). The biographer records Einstein's answer to the question of what schools should emphasize: "In teaching history, there should be extensive discussion of personalities who benefited mankind through independence of character and judgment" (p. 6). Isaacson elaborates:

> At a time when there is a new emphasis, in the face of global competition, on science and math education, we should also note the other part of Einstein's answer. "Critical comments by students should be taken in a friendly spirit," he said. "Accumulation of material should not stifle the student's independence." A society's competitive advantage will come not from how well its schools teach the multiplication and periodic tables, but from how well they stimulate imagination and creativity. (pp. 6–7)

Einstein did not do well with rote learning, finding school a distraction from his need to be creative and imaginative. Indeed, his famous thought experiments, which led to the theory of relativity, were a process of independent thinking and discovery, a learning strategy we would do well to prioritize. To engage, teachers ask good questions that ignite creativity and imagination.

Final Thoughts

An overarching pedagogy for all teachers is to cause *engaged* learning. In the best of situations, teachers and learners journey together toward transformational goals. A sense of mutual transformation is not meant to romanticize the partnership, but it is stated to encourage knowing individual learners and empowering them to reach their goals. We need to connect to the experiences of the learners themselves. Guided inquiry teaching provides an ideal pedagogy because it creates relevant connections to students' lives. Our teacher toolbox contains a powerful instrument: the question. Questions can be used to discover how much students know, assess their progress, gauge the depth of their understanding, promote thinking, and aid the transfer of knowledge into new contexts. Guided inquiry teaching provides many opportunities for teacher-student collaboration. These approaches honor students' learning skills, their experiences, and their innate interests as learners. The demand on the teacher to provide the necessary resources and structure for reaching conclusions may seem daunting. The temptation to use a conventional deductive method to expedite information is always tempting. However, the values of some form of inquiry teaching are manifold, especially if authentic practice is used. Few approaches provide more tangible results of comprehension, reflection, and problem-solving skills. Teachers have the benefit of observing the learning process as it evolves and is refined, and they can better use a mentoring influence to inspire. Both process and product are rewarded.

EPILOGUE

A colleague shared a story with us about one of our freshman students on his way to an 8 a.m. class. He poked his head into the teacher's office and asked if she had a coffee cup she could share. The professor, Dr. Ann Singleton, said that the school had a stock of Styrofoam cups just around the corner. He said, "No, I prefer a ceramic cup. Do you have one?" The professor recognized his attitude as one of the unflattering parts of a generation of students who are used to barking their orders into a speaker at McDonald's and getting what they want quickly. How do we teach such students?

Indeed, another generation is fast upon their heels, the postmillennials, what some have called the "iGeneration" (Jayson, 2010). For this generation, it is *all* about technology constantly connecting them to the world. It is the same desire for individualized immediacy as their older counterparts, only supersized. How do we *cope* with students who send text messages and use the Internet in class while claiming they are indeed paying attention?

Our response has been multifaceted because we think teaching is a complicated process. We have written that pedagogy is about inspiration, whole teachers, whole learners, and placing students at its center. We have also said that our intentions are for naught if we do not teach for learning, know how our learners learn, focus more on the pedagogy of process, and use the power of questions in the classroom. In a word, our book is about change in education.

The Information Age is not our enemy. Its wonders undoubtedly are assets in our schools and in education. Students and teachers can access rich resources of knowledge and motivation. For example, while less common in P–12 schools (Miller, 2010), higher education has been using YouTube EDU for some time to post courses or video lessons online for students. More common is the use of sites like TeacherTube, a service designed for teachers. Great teachers learn from and adapt to the present while holding on to ideas and concepts that they know are transformational. In teaching, the past can be even more valuable than the present and future because we can study it and learn from it. Technology is changing the way our students view our teaching and our classrooms, and it is changing the way teachers view teaching.

We recognize impatience in our students and in ourselves as we conform to our fast-paced society. This century's material and emotional temptations can affect us the way too many toys for Christmas affects young children. After a while the child cannot focus on any one toy and even develops a certain indifference to the whole pile of toys. Wise parents quickly put away most of the toys for another day, allowing their children to enjoy each one more thoroughly.

This book has aimed to re-create school through the eyes of the transformational teacher. But we cannot re-create or transform if we are too busy conforming. How do we adapt to the fast-paced lifestyles we all lead or feel compelled to live? The quick and easy route seems programmed into human nature, often leading to impetuous conformity.

We can see at least two manifestations of this impatience in education. One is the quick and easy reliance upon a single, highly consequential indicator, the test score, for measuring effectiveness in education. Rothstein, Wilder, and Jacobsen (2007) describe our educational system as "overemphasizing basic skills—not because we don't know any better, but because we want accountability on the cheap" (p. 14). We need to move beyond a single indicator of performance to holistic assessment.

A second manifestation of 21st century impatience in education is the propensity to pander to the gods of technology and entertainment. Neil Postman (1999), who was often accused of being a neo-Luddite, said being anti-technology would be something like being anti-food—we need it to live. But we can eat too much food, or we can eat bad food—and the analogy surely applies to how we often view technology. Luddites were skilled garment workers in early 19th century England who violently resisted the mechanization of their industry because they saw it would ruin their way of life. Postman sees "nothing irrational about loser-resistance" (p. 46). He then attempted to put our fast-paced society into perspective.

He posited that the 19th century was where we learned how to invent things while an understanding of why we did various things receded in importance. Postman raises a simple but profound issue related to technological change in the late 20th century leading into this era: "What is the problem to which this technology is the solution?" (p. 42). It is an important question to consider if we desire teaching that is transformational.

It is more than tempting in this age of technology and fast-paced decision making to seek to engage this generation of students by thinking that technology is a substitute for thinking, and that entertainment is synonymous with active learning. Ravitch (2000) terms such thinking as a society that tolerates anti-intellectualism in schools and a "dumbed-down culture that honors celebrity and sensation rather than knowledge and wisdom" (p. 460). The issue of equating entertainment with education is a salient one for all teachers in the 21st century. Teachers who try to exploit or compete with the speed of the latest gadgets in technology and communication have lost their focus, and will probably not succeed in the heart and science of teaching.

Balance

Despite our anxieties surrounding the overuse of technology in education and modern culture, we do believe in striking a livable balance. Learners who have grown up with new ways of accessing information, new modes of informal learning related to their social lives, and new tools for joining a community of lifelong learning should be encouraged to explore lively and inspiring new ways of learning (Davidson, 2007). We must be careful to avoid the divisive word *or* in education. Technology and media are wonderful tools when used to inspire reflection, social interaction, and individual intellectual accountability. What continues to be missing, however, is attention to the whole person's deep understanding as illuminated by synergistic academic, social, and spiritual educational opportunities.

Education is a partnership among stakeholders, especially school and home and teacher and student. The purpose of education is to free individuals to become the kinds of persons they can and need to become. Holism can be a liberating force. Indeed, as per ASCD's Whole Child Initiative, it can "redefine what a successful learner is and how we measure success."

If we continue to promote a great divide between the goals of the head and heart in public schools, our society will not access the greater good that higher expectations accomplish. The Transformational Pedagogy Model includes academic, social, and spiritual goals. Connecting these goals creates a vital force in both education and in life (Trueblood, 1996), pointing more toward consensus than division; more toward comprehensiveness than singularity; and more toward not just mind, but mind and soul. The past is important to understanding the future. Educators through the ages made the following connections:

- Plato: matter *and* ideas
- Aristotle: reason *and* virtue
- Aquinas: spiritual *and* rational thought
- Erasmus: knowledge of words *and* knowledge of truth
- Dewey: school *and* society
- Piaget: physical *and* social environment

- Bruner: process *and* product
- Gardner: thinking *and* feeling
- Jobs and Gates: immediacy *and* customization

As we learn to adapt and compete in the global marketplace, we can also seek our spiritual summons. Our vocations need not be empty of meaning. We need not live "lives of quiet desperation" as Thoreau suggested, as though hopelessness is imposed by society's circumstances and fears.

Learning from Our Past

The challenges of the 21st century are similar to other periods when tumultuous events occurred. Evolving technologies, culture shock, new problems with unknown parameters and solutions, and disruption of societal and moral absolutes are all examples of profound change in the human experience.

Benjamin Franklin has been called the "first American" for many reasons. Franklin lived during the century of the American Revolution and was an inventor, writer, philosopher, scientist, entrepreneur, and politician. But mostly Franklin was the first American because he embodied the independent, indefatigable curiosity of spirit that inspires so many people. In 1751, Franklin created the Philadelphia Academy because he saw a need in colonial society for citizens to adjust to changing culture. The old ways of the Latin Grammar School were not sufficient for colonists who needed to know languages besides Latin and Greek, to learn basic geography and history, and mathematical and science skills of the new age of the 18th century, and who lacked critical thinking skills attuned to the challenging demands of modernism. Sound familiar?

Global challenges to our educational methods are not unprecedented, though they are different. U.S. schools are not adequately preparing graduates to meet global challenges. The solution, however, has become part of the problem. Marge Scherer (2005) brings us sharply into focus by asking:

> If you asked Aristotle, John Dewey, and Martin Luther King, Jr., to describe the aims of education, would they offer any version of the education

goals that drive U.S. public schools today? Would any world-class visionary identify proficiency in basic skills as the primary aim for every student? Would he or she declare adequate yearly progress a school's central
reason for being? (p. 7)

Perhaps we need a 21st century Franklin Plan where a unique
response to the Information Age can be developed and where traditional but relevant life skills like creativity, empathy, practicality,
respect for rights and individuality, work ethic, moral responsibility,
and honesty are always welcome in our schools.

Foundational Thoughts

We have sought to explore the teacher-student dynamic through
an analysis of pedagogy. We have engaged our study at the individual
level, while exploring the potential of whole teachers teaching the
whole learner. It now seems appropriate to synthesize and apply our
thoughts to a larger view of education. The following are our foundational priorities for the future of modern education.

We have to get along with each other. Teamwork is increasingly
the mode of operation for the workplace, and new technologies can
assist us. Pedagogy that demands communication, cooperation, and
collaboration is necessary. Just the English language alone contains
over 540,000 words, five times the amount in Shakespeare's day, with
many of the new words being technical-speak (Fisch, 2008). Cultural
competence includes the ability to communicate in different languages, but it also is values laden. Individual goal structures that pre-
clude social and cultural awareness will not be tolerated.

Students must be allowed to shoulder responsibility for their
learning. Fareed Zakaria (2006) demonstrates that independent, creative thinking has been a strength of our country's people, admired
by many, including Asian countries like Singapore, which has led the
world in math and science achievement scores. But such daring does
not thrive in the contemporary back-to-basics culture in the United
States. Critical thinking, learning how to learn, synthesizing big
ideas for the real world, and learning how to solve problems that are

relevant to students and to society make for powerful pedagogy. It is indeed ironic, educationally speaking, that the United States is emulating Singapore while Singapore wants to be like the United States. We live in a country where we enjoy a way of life that gives dignity to all. Schools are the transformers for democracy. But maximum dignity can only be realized in a transforming relationship when we stop de-prioritizing (and, coincidingly, entitling) the student, the most critical stakeholder in our schools. Low test scores are the responsibility of all, including and especially our students.

Classrooms must be learner-centered environments. Bransford et al. (2000) describe learning environments that are fourfold in focus: learner centered, knowledge centered, community centered, and assessment centered. These four environments are not mutually exclusive; they all have something to offer. Classrooms must connect to the learners' experiences; they must connect to knowledge and community to ensure transfer from the context of school to the context of society. Classrooms must be established where formative assessment is viewed as part of instruction. While all four are needed, however, learner centered as a focus is the most pedagogically vital of the four because our students are not just who but why we teach, constituting our fundamental mission in schooling.

Great teachers are needed more than ever. Our students must do the learning, but they need the assistance of transformational teachers. Ravitch (2000) reminds us that "technology can supplement schooling but not replace it; even the most advanced electronic technologies are incapable of turning their worlds of information into mature knowledge" (p. 460). Great teachers work hard to prepare in their subject and in their methodology. They also use their emotional and spiritual resources as they relate to their students' needs. The best teachers are not interested in telling their learners what to think; instead, they focus on teaching processes that encourage and enable students' thinking. Students need an authoritative, balanced perspective from their teachers based on mature knowledge and a transcendent standard. Students must see that their teacher is committed to that standard.

The educational challenges of this century can be placed in perspective. Walter Isaacson (2007) writes about Albert Einstein's worldview of individuality toward science and life in a context of reverence for the transcendent:

> Beneath all of his theories, including relativity, was a quest for invariants, certainties, and absolutes. There was a harmonious reality underlying the laws of the universe, Einstein felt, and the goal of science was to discover it. (p. 3)

This quest was made by an imaginative nonconformist:

> This outlook made Einstein a rebel with a reverence for the harmony of nature, one who had just the right blend of imagination and wisdom to transform our understanding of the universe. These traits are just as vital for this new century of globalization, in which our success will depend on our creativity, as they were for the beginning of the twentieth century, when Einstein helped usher in the modern age. (p. 7)

Schools throughout time have succeeded and failed in the quest for liberating the potential of the human spirit. A quest for holism in education unlocks the potential for inspiration and deeper learning that can transform our students. We can have it all in teaching and learning *if* we seek it.

A New Clock

Teaching didactically can be quite problematic, even frustrating. In order to convince ourselves that teaching for coverage of knowledge is futile, we would like to put in perspective the clockface metaphor taken from Neil Postman and Charles Weingartner's (1969) writings presented at the beginning of this book.

If we started a new clock for the future, what would it look like? Twelve seconds from now we will have eight billion humans on Earth, and futurists (Pulliam & Van Patten, 2007) predict that humans will travel by light beam. Thirty seconds from now, we will have mind-to-mind communication. Whether these predictions come to be or not, it is clear that we are living in a wondrous digital age. Bill Gates believes that technological change will affect society and its educational institutions as much as any discovery in human history. We do not believe his statement is farfetched. We can expect that this century will be at least as different from the 20th as the 20th was different from the 19th century. The wisdom and knowledge of the past must be preserved as we engage with students this century.

Final Thoughts

Education has the power to transform lives, and teachers are the catalysts for such a transformation. We teach by who we are more than by what we say. What we believe makes a difference in why we teach, in how we teach, in what we teach, and ultimately in whom we teach. As we consider whom we teach, we recall the idea that it is the way learners feel in school that transcends curricula. The academic, the social, and the spiritual belong together. Emotion illuminates cognition and memory.

One of the most enthralling scenes produced in a movie can be found in *Immortal Beloved* (1994), about the inspired life of Ludwig van Beethoven. The scene is a flashback to the troubled composer's childhood, where he escapes his upstairs room, flees from his abusive father, runs through the woods to a shallow pond, strips to his undergarments, lies on his back in the water facing the starry heavens, and hears in his mind the genius of the strains of the Ninth Symphony's *Ode to Joy*. We are changed as we watch and listen and comprehend the sheer power and transcendence of the scene. Illumination can occur when learners connect to the whole.

Transformational pedagogy shouts, "No good teacher teaches the same course or lesson twice." It is holistic teaching with the learner in the center. We teach students, and they are always different. We are spiritual bridges to learners, to their needs, to their sometimes desperate lives. Our schools need to be places where transformation is a daily reality.

APPENDIX: TEACHING STORIES

S uccessful classrooms include flexibility, creativity, high expectations, and indeed, a certain community of mutuality. What
follows are a few teaching stories from educators that focus
on the transformation of the teacher and the learner, in classrooms
at all levels of education. We were interested in the role these educators played as teachers, what was taught, what the learners did,
and how the teacher and learner interacted and responded in the
classroom. We asked them to share an anecdote from their teaching
careers where something special academically, socially, or spiritually
occurred in their classroom or school.

Trusting Students to Learn

I am a veteran teacher, but only recently added my philosophy of
teaching on the course syllabus. Unfortunately, it has taken years for
me to feel confident that my philosophy of teaching is both authentic and informed. My philosophy changed significantly from what
teachers do to a group of students to how teachers can design a classroom where individual students can learn. Trusting that my students

could and would learn is a significant presupposition, essential for this more effective teaching style that is student focused. The refinement of my teaching style did not come easily to me; however, learning to trust my students has proven to be mutually transforming in both my life and the lives of my students.

I began teaching with an emphasis on controlling the environment of my students and, yes, trying to control the behaviors of my students. Whether the teaching environment was a public school classroom, a children's choir at church, or a college classroom, I was in control. I spent hours planning what these groups of students would do, when they would it, and exactly how long it would take them to do it. Having some success with my teaching, I became comfortable with this teaching style. It was too many years later that I was introduced to the more dynamic approach to teaching associated with brain-based learning.

As I began to understand more about how our brains operate and the conditions that facilitate learning, I began asking more questions and listening to my students. I encouraged them to talk to each other as I gave them time to think. I let them control the pace of the class and gave them choices about instructional content and design. The results were astonishing.

I remember changing the way that I was teaching the concept of lesson planning, a rather overwhelming process that includes goals, objectives, assessments, directions for activities, and specific age-appropriate language. In earlier years of teaching, I made a presentation that included logical explanations, clarifying examples, and amusing anecdotes. I enjoyed giving the presentation, but my students' first lesson plans were always disappointing. They didn't grasp even the basic elements of a well-planned lesson; consequently, we would spend many hours laboriously writing individual parts of a lesson plan during class time.

As I learned more about teaching from the perspective of facilitating students' learning rather than controlling students' learning, I decided to approach my teaching of lesson planning differently. I spent more time introducing the process of planning and allowing my students to experience its importance. Then, I gave them a packet of materials that gave them important information to help them plan a lesson and three well-planned lessons for them to see. These more recent students turned in lesson plans that demonstrated a much better understanding of the planning process. I was learning that when I can trust my students with their learning, they will learn more.

Learning to trust my students with their learning has made a broader contribution to the community of learning than just in my classroom. I remember an excellent student in my beginning years in higher education. She was a bright student with a heart for students with disabilities, and I knew that she would make a significant contribution to my profession.

Unfortunately, personal circumstances kept her from graduating for 18 years. As a part of finishing her degree, she needed to take a methods course by directed study. Traditionally, this course is not even considered as one that can be taught independently. A mentor encouraged me to allow this student the trust requisite for an independent learning experience. She earned an *A*; however, the true test of her learning was her first teaching assignment: teaching mathematics to 18 5th and 6th grade students in special education. All students scored at the 1st grade level at the beginning of the school year. By the end of the year, her students' scores on mathematics achievement tests ranged from grade 3 to grade 5, with one student testing on grade level. That's confirmation that students deserve the opportunity to learn without having to meet traditional artificial requirements for a particular course.

As I have learned to trust my students and plan accordingly, my philosophy of teaching has developed into a more informed one, a philosophy that I now can profess with confidence:

- Teaching only takes place when learning has occurred.
- A good teacher facilitates the process of learning by using a myriad of practices.
- Teaching practices range from an engaging presentation to opportunities that prompt meaningful discussion and student interaction.

• The emphasis of teaching is all about supporting the students' understanding of the key issues.

• Effective teaching results in both students and teachers leaving the classroom with an appreciation for the concepts discussed, coupled with a feeling of empowerment that supports deep thinking about those concepts.

• The best teachers learn from their students and never cease to learn.

Ann Singleton, Higher Education and Special Education

Hugs and Hearing

I teach students who are deaf and hard of hearing. My first five years of teaching were in a residential school setting in a behavioral classroom, designed for students whose behaviors were too disruptive for placement in the regular classroom and cottage settings. I was hired to teach elementary students, a group of educational and social outcasts that most adults had given up on and few students had attempted to maintain friendships with. As the teacher, my focus was more on behavior than on academics: I worked with the students to develop appropriate strategies for handling stressful situations. I was ill prepared for the task.

One student had extremely difficult, and often dangerous, behaviors. She had daily temper tantrums that included throwing objects at staff and other students, overturning desks and chairs, repeatedly slamming doors, hitting, kicking, pinching, scratching, and spitting. Her actions would usually escalate from slamming her fists on her desk to something as dangerous as chasing after another student with a sharp object. During my first year, her behavior was harmful enough to herself or to others that my assistant and I would need to physically restrain her until she had calmed down.

I remember that she would look at me from the corner of her eye to see my reaction when she showed her middle finger to another student in the classroom. She tried to make me flinch by pulling her fist back. I can remember her slamming the door to the "time-out" room until an adult stood by the doorway. I remember days when she would run out of the classroom because she was angry but return to the classroom because I hadn't chased her.

Mostly, though, I remember a particularly difficult day. The student was having repeated behavioral outbursts that required attention. In the midst of one temper tantrum, my assistant, who was seated, calmly asked, "Do you want a hug?" The student immediately stopped what she was doing and burst into tears. My assistant, still seated, put out her arms and the student curled up in her lap and cried for several minutes.

I had recognized that the student exhibited attention-seeking behaviors, and I had been working with her on more acceptable ways to get attention. I had failed to realize how truly desperate she had become. With that one hug, I realized that she was willing to do absolutely anything to get attention. As with many kids, her disruptive behaviors were designed to attract attention. Refusing to do an assignment, which may result in less free time, was worth the one-on-one attention that she would receive while completing the work. Slamming the time-out room's door, which would result in being isolated in the room longer, was worth it to have a staff member stand nearby in the doorway. But most depressing to me was the realization that attacking another student or attempting to injure herself, which would result in multiple days of lost privileges, was worth the physical touch that she would receive while being restrained.

Disruptive behavior and defiance could no longer simply be attributed to a lack of social skills. These were covert cries for help. I began trying to give her the attention that she so desperately needed before she began seeking it through inappropriate behaviors. The first time she refused to follow a request, I began asking about her weekend. I held her hand when we walked to lunch, and I carried her on my back as we ran to P.E. Most important, I continued to ask her if she needed a hug.

Over the course of the next three school years, I only had to restrain her one more time. She taught me that my job as her teacher was to connect to who she was. She changed when I changed.

Tom Stanton, Deaf Education

Honest Connections

When I was given the opportunity to teach a course in voice and diction, I designed the course to be student centered. The students and I explored the nature of voice and diction and the practice of it in their lives and experiences. Everyone, including myself, was growing and developing a stronger sense of the important role our voices play as tools for presenting our messages to others. At the six-week mark, through a wide variety of student activities and the occasional informal lectures, we had developed a pleasant rapport and a shared sense of trust. While a good rapport is important in effective learning, trust is critical in creating an atmosphere for safe learning. Trust is especially critical in public performance courses in which students engage an audience with messages that communicate their ideas, beliefs, and values. Having gauged where we were, I determined that it was time for our first examination.

I designed a traditional exam that was predominately objective with some opportunity for essay. I considered it a fair exam and administered it to my students. I believe in giving prompt feedback to students, so I began grading the tests the same afternoon. After grading the first five exams, I was dismayed by the low scores. My students often have their lowest grades on the first exam, but the average is usually a high *C* or low *B*. These tests were nowhere near that mark; the average of everyone's grade was in the low 60s—an average I found unacceptable.

Throughout that evening and into the next day, I thought about what had happened. I thought about the role that the students played in earning these grades. Perhaps they hadn't studied enough; perhaps they didn't take the class seriously. I went through a long list of possibilities regarding the students, and then turned the spotlight on me. Perhaps I hadn't prepared the students well enough for the test; perhaps the course design, primarily activities based, hadn't translated to an objective test. After much reflection, I came to the conclusion that perhaps the latter was the case.

I had designed the course and hadn't adequately prepared the students for understanding what I expected them to demonstrate on the exam. At the next class period, I walked in with my red test folder and told my students that I was disappointed in the examination results. I am certain my students were afraid that would be the case. They were quiet, serious, and looked concerned about their grades. I continued to say that I was disappointed in the examination results because I felt that I had failed the students in giving that *particular* exam. I told them that I felt I hadn't equipped them well enough for the exam. I also told them that I had considered the possibility that they hadn't prepared well for the exam, and while that may have been true, I believed that I bore the greatest responsibility for the low scores.

I felt that the low results were at least 75 percent my fault. I sincerely apologized for the fact that I had unintentionally let them down and caused them unnecessary worry. The students rushed to my defense and told me that they were more to blame than 25 percent. I was pleased by their loyalty, but I told them that "mistakes are made, people fail, and life goes on. It is how one handles these failures and mistakes that matters." I was open to learning from this mistake because it would help inform my teaching and, more importantly, I could prevent this from happening to my students again. After asking for suggestions from them on how we might proceed in regard to the exam grades, we hammered out a workable plan. Everyone was in agreement, and the class sailed on.

What I find interesting is the transformation that took place for both me and my students. Unfortunately, students have an expectation that a poor test result will be blamed on them, and possibly all too often that does happen. They were amazed when I walked in to class and said, "This test didn't work. It was my fault. I am sorry. Let me try again!" I think the students felt empowered in the understanding that we were on this journey together and that I could make mistakes and publicly admit it.

The class and I grew even closer after the experience. They felt safe in the knowledge that I had their best interests at heart and that I wasn't going to put my own pride above their success. My students and I were transformed because this experience cemented the fact that power in the classroom was not linked to the end of my pen. Instead, the power was linked to making honest connections with each other, trusting each other, making mistakes, and moving forward together.

Teresa Collard, Higher Education

GLOSSARY

Gleaned from the book are definitions of words in the categories of educational philosophy, psychology, and pedagogy.

Philosophy

Arête—virtue for Aristotle

Core values—patterns of attitudes and behaviors that assist with meeting human needs and resolving conflicts between individuals and groups

Divine and—a focus on the more inclusive conjunction with dualisms in philosophy, psychology, education, and theology

Essentialism—a traditional philosophy of education that emphasizes building upon basic subjects in schooling

Fifth dimension—a reality of the spiritual beyond space (length, width, depth) and time

Philosophy—a system of thinking that deals with ultimate questions of truth, reality, and goodness

Teaching philosophy: (a) progressive philosophies—a set of educational philosophies prioritizing the learner's needs for learning and a more flexible role for the teacher; (b) traditional philosophies—a set of educational philosophies that prioritize subject matter and a traditional role for the teacher

Psychology

Accommodation—the process in learning theory of changing a schema in response to the assimilation of discrepant stimuli

Assimilation—the process in learning theory of taking information into an existing schema

Behavioral psychology—focuses on learners as motivated by external forces in the learning environment

Cognitive psychology—focuses on learners as mentally, emotionally, and physically active

Curiosity—an innate need to know in learners

Disequilibrium—a mental discomfort or dissonance that is a response to inexplicable or confounding events in the learning environment

Hot cognition—a phenomenon with memory in which learners pay more attention to content with emotional overtones

Learning sciences—the study of learning in real-world learning environments with the goal of providing a sound scientific foundation for education

Locus of control—placing the cause or control of events to factors within one's self or outside one's self

Multiple intelligences—Gardner's term for a set of abilities or aptitudes individual to learners and conceptualized as subject matter or content related

Others and objects—social and physical factors, respectively, in the environment that are sources of new knowledge

Plasticity—the brain's adaptability to new and different circumstances and experiences

Psychology—the study of mental processes and behavior

Schema—a structure in the brain in learning theory for the collection of knowledge

Self-efficacy—a belief in one's own capability to succeed

Situated cognition—learning that is tied (situated) to the learning environment and concern for the learning context

Sociocultural learning—a theory by Vygotsky where teacher support is critical

Transfer of learning—where knowledge is applied in another context or in a new way

Zone of proximal development—Vygotsky's term for the gap between learners' level of achievement and the demands of the curriculum

Pedagogy

Academic domains—arbitrary but functional collections of knowledge in institutionalized fields that we call subjects

Academic goals—learning ends that spring from traditional liberal arts and professional education

Active learning—cognitive and social growth fostered by engagement in activities

Advance organizers—Ausubel's term for introductory cues or materials that assist learners in organizing their learning

Attention—learners' ability to observe, listen, and concentrate mentally

Authentic practice—learning activities in an applied, real-world context

Brain-based learning—a process of creating a learning environment (challenge, novelty, meaning, feedback, repetition, emotion) where the brain seems to learn best

Catechetical method—classical, Christian school pedagogy of reading, memorizing, and reciting

Constructivism—a pedagogical theory where learners are viewed as capable of constructing their own knowledge with guidance from the teacher

Coverage—a teaching approach focusing on breadth instead of depth of knowledge

Discussion—the verbal interaction between teacher and learners, and learners with learners

Engaged learning—pedagogy that connects to experiences of learners

Experience—what the learner already knows

Exposition—the presentation of subject matter to learners by a teacher or media/technology source

Folk pedagogy—Bruner's term for the use of everyday, intuitive theories to explain how learners learn

Formative assessment—systematic efforts to assess learning in process in order to monitor student progress/growth

Heart and science of education—a focus on feelings and fulfillment along with rational, clear thinking

Holistic education—a focus on the head, heart, and hands with the goal of producing healthy, fulfilled, and participating citizens

Illumination—a moment of insight for a learner as a potential solution or understanding suddenly comes into awareness

Informational teaching—a pedagogy that teaches for the assimilation of information: schooling centered on teaching for coverage of knowledge

Inquiry teaching—a guided discovery approach to teaching and learning that utilizes problem solving and the scientific method

Pedagogy—the art and science of teaching and learning

Postholing—a pedagogy where teachers pause to "dig in" for deep understanding

Problems-based learning—a pedagogy that matches curriculum with problem solving

Service learning—a distinct, intentional pedagogy that expands learners' experiences by combining curriculum, real-world altruistic application, and reflection

Social goals—learning ends that are designed to better human welfare

Spiritual goals—learning ends that deal with principles of eternal values, transcending the material and temporal

Transformational Pedagogy Model—a system of goals and roles designed synergistically to change the learner academically, socially, and spiritually

Transformational teaching—a pedagogy that teaches for change with convictions about holism and deeper understanding in learning goals

Whole child—conceiving and perceiving learners as a whole academically, physically, emotionally, socially, and spiritually

REFERENCES

Adolphs, R., & Damasion, A. (2001). The interaction of affect and cognition: A neurobiological perspective. In J. P. Forgas (Ed.), *Handbook of affect and social cognition* (pp. 27–49). Mahwah, NJ: Erlbaum.

Alexander, P. (2006). *Psychology in learning and instruction.* Upper Saddle River, NJ: Merrill/Pearson Education.

Armstrong, T. (2007). The curriculum superhighway. *Educational Leadership, 64*(8), 16–20.

ASCD. (n.d.) The whole child initiative. Retrieved October 29, 2010, from http://www.ascd.org/programs/The-Whole-Child/The-Whole-Child.aspx.

Ausubel, D. P. (1968). *Educational psychology: A cognitive view.* New York: Holt, Rinehart and Winston.

Barr, R., & Tagg, J. (1995). From teaching to learning: A new paradigm for undergraduate education. In D. DeZure (Ed.), (2000), *Learning from change: Landmarks in teaching and learning in higher education from Change Magazine, 1969–1999* (pp. 198–200). Sterling, VA: Stylus Publishing.

Bauerlein, M. (2008). *The dumbest generation: How the digital age stupefies young Americans and jeopardizes our future.* London: Penguin.

Beyer, B. (1971). *Inquiry in the social studies classroom: A strategy for teaching.* Columbus: Merrill.

Bjork, R., & Richardson-Klavhen, A. (1989). On the puzzling relationship between environment context and human memory. In C. Izawa (Ed.), *Current issues in cognitive processes: The Tulane flowerree symposium on cognition.* Hillsdale, NJ: Erlbaum.

Blumenfeld, P., Kempler, T., & Krajcik, J. (2006). Motivation and cognitive engagement in learning environments. In R. K. Sawyer (Ed.), *The Cambridge handbook of learning sciences*. New York: Cambridge University Press.

Blumenfeld, P., Soloway, E., Marx, R. W., Krajcik, J. S., Guzdial, M., & Palincsar, A. (1991). Motivating project-based learning: Sustaining the doing, supporting the learning. *Educational Psychologist, 26,* 369–398.

Braham, J. (2006). *The light within the light: Portraits of Donald Hall, Richard Wilbur, Maxine Kumin, and Stanley Kunitz.* Jeffery, NH: David R. Godine.

Bransford, J., Brown, A., & Cocking, R. (Eds.). (2000). *How people learn: Brain, mind, experience, and school.* Washington, DC: National Academy Press.

Breault, D. (2005). Work in school. In D. Breault & R. Breault (Eds.), (pp. 18–20). *Experiencing Dewey.* Indianapolis: Kappa Delta Pi.

Bredo, E. (2006). Conceptual confusion and educational psychology. In P. A. Alexander & P. H. Winne (Eds.), *Handbook of educational psychology* (2nd ed., pp. 43–57). Mahwah, NJ: Erlbaum.

Brooks, J. G. (2004). To see beyond the lesson. *Educational Leadership, 62*(1), 9–12.

Brophy, J. E. (1990). Probing the subtleties of subject-matter teaching. *Educational Leadership, 49*(7), 4–8.

Bruner, J. (1974). *Relevance of education.* New York: Penguin.

Bruner, J. (1996). *The culture of education.* Cambridge, MA: Harvard University Press.

Bruning, R. H., Shaw, G. B., & Ronning, R. R. (2004). *Cognitive psychology and instruction* (4th ed.). Upper Saddle River, NJ: Merrill/Pearson Education.

Byrnes, J. (2001). *Minds, brains, and learning: Understanding the psychological and education relevance of neuroscientific research.* New York: Guilford Press.

Cahill, L., Haier, R., Fallon, J., Alkire, M., Tang, C., Keator, D., Wu, J., & McGaugh, J. (1996). Amygdala activity at encoding correlated with long-term, free recall of emotional information. *Proceedings of the National Academy of Sciences, 93,* 8016–8321.

Campbell, D. (2008, September 10). Plugging in, tuning out. *USA Today,* p. 11A.

Carr, M., & Biddlecomb, B. (1998). Metacognition in mathematics from a constructivist perspective. In D. J. Hacker, J. Dunlosky, & A. C. Graesser (Eds.), *Metacognition in educational theory and practice.* (pp. 69–91). Mahwah, NJ: Erlbaum.

Carr, N. (2008, July/August). Is Google making us stupid? *The Atlantic,* 58.

Casals, P. (1970). *Joys and sorrows: Reflections.* New York: Simon & Schuster.

Castro-Caldas, A., Miranda, P., Carmo, I., Reis, A., Leote, F., Ribeiro, C., & Ducla-Soares, E. (1999). Influence of learning to read and write on the morphology of the corpus callosum. *European Journal of Neurology, 6,* 23–28.

Chen, Z. (1999). Schema induction in children's analogical problem solving. *Journal of Educational Psychology, 91,* 703–715.

Cheshier, T. (2010, January 8). Snow days cause TCAP test worries for teachers. *The Jackson Sun,* 1.

Cobb, P., & Bowers, J. (1999). Cognitive and situated learning perspectives in theory and practice. *Educational Researcher, 28*(2), 4–15.

Collins, A. (2006). Cognitive apprenticeship. In R. K. Sawyer (Ed.), *The Cambridge handbook of the learning sciences* (pp. 47–60). New York: Cambridge University Press.

Collins, R. R. (2009). Taking care of one another. *Educational Leadership, 66*(8), 81–82.

Cormier, S., & Hagman, J. (1987). Introduction. In S. Cormier & J. Hagman (Eds.), *Transfer of learning: Contemporary research and applications*. San Diego: Academic Press.

Cranton, P. (2002). Teaching for transformation. *New Directions for Adult and Continuing Education, 93*, 63–71.

Davidson, C. (2007). We can't ignore the influence of digital technologies. *The Chronicle of Higher Education, 53*(29), B20.

DeWar, G. (2009). Teaching empathy: Evidence-based tips for fostering empathy in children. *Parenting Science*. Retrieved January 2010 from http://www.parenting science.com/teaching-empathy-tips.html

Dewey, J. (1938). *Experience and education*. New York: Macmillan.

DiMartino, J., & Clarke, J. H. (2008). *Personalizing the high school experience for each student*. Alexandria, VA: ASCD.

diSessa, A. A. (2006). A history of conceptual change research: Threads and fault lines. In R. K. Sawyer (Ed.), *The Cambridge handbook of the learning sciences*. New York: Cambridge University Press.

Dockery, D. (2008). *Renewing minds: Serving church and society through Christian higher education*. Nashville, TN: B & H Publishing Group.

Doyle, T. (2008). *Helping students learn in a learner-centered environment*. Sterling, VA: Stylus Publishing.

Eisner, E. (2005). Back to whole. *Educational Leadership, 63*(1), 14–18.

Elbert, T., Pantev, C., Wienbruch, C., Rockstroh, B., & Taub, E. (1995). Increased cortical representation of the fingers of the left hand in string players. *Science, 270*, 305–307.

Ericsson, K., Krampe, R., & Tesch-Romer, C. (1993). The role of deliberate practice in the acquisition of expert performance. *Psychological Review, 100*, 363–406.

Esquith, R. (2007). *Teach like your hair's on fire: The methods and madness inside room 56*. New York: Penguin Group.

Eysenck, M. (1992). *Anxiety: The cognitive perspective*. Hove, England: Erlbaum.

Fisch, K. (2008). Retrieved March 2008 from www.youtube.com/watch?V=pMcfr LYDm2U.

Friedman, T. L. (2007). *The world is flat: A brief history of the twenty-first century* (Rev. ed.). New York: Picador.

Gardner, H. (1999). *Intelligence reframed: Multiple intelligences for the 21st century*. New York: Basic Books.

Gardner, H., Csikszentmihalyi, M., & Damon, W. (2001). *Good work: When excellence and ethics meet*. New York: Basic Books.

Glaser, R. (1992). Expert knowledge and processes of thinking. In D. Halpern (Ed.), *Enhancing thinking skills in the sciences and mathematics* (pp. 63–75). Hillsdale, NJ: Erlbaum.

Goodwin, D. (2005). *Team of rivals*. New York: Simon & Schuster.

Gordon, G., with Crabtree, S. (2006). *Building engaged schools: Getting the most out of America's classrooms*. Princeton, NJ: Gallup Press.

Greenough, W., Black, J., & Volkmar, F. (1979). Maze training effects on dendritic branching in occipital cortex of adult rats. *Behavioral and Neural Biology, 26*, 287–297.

Harvey, B. (1999). *Another city: An ecclesiological primer for a post-Christian world*. Philadelphia: Trinity Press International.

Hattie, J. (1992). Measuring the effects of schooling. *Australian Journal of Education, 36*(1), 5–13.

Helm, J. H. (2004). Projects that power young minds. *Educational Leadership, 62*(1), 58–62.

Hobin, M. (1974). Clarifying what's important. In A. O. Kownslar (Ed.), *American history: The quest for relevancy* (169–187). Washington, DC: National Council for the Social Studies.

Hoffman, M. (1991). Empathy, social cognition, and moral action. In W. M. Kurtines & J. Gewirtz (Eds.), *Moral behavior and development: Vol. 1, Theory*. Hillsdale, NJ: Erlbaum.

Hood, L. (2009). Platooning instruction: Districts weigh pros and cons of departmentalizing elementary schools. Retrieved October 2009 from http://www.hepg.org/hel/article/426

Houghton, J. (2006). *Bill Moyers on faith and reason*. Films for the Humanities and Sciences. Princeton, NJ: Films Media Group.

Huebner, D. (Ed.). (1999). *The lure of the transcendent: Collected essays by Dwayne E. Huebner*. Mahwah, NJ: Erlbaum.

Intrator, S. M. (2004). The engaged classroom. *Educational Leadership, 62*(1), 20–25.

Isaacson, W. (2007). *Einstein: His life and universe*. New York: Simon & Schuster.

Jackson, R. R. (2009). *Never work harder than your students & other principles of great teaching*. Alexandria, VA: ASCD.

Jayson, S. (2010, February 10). iGeneration has no off switch. *USA Today*, pp. 1D–2D.

Joyce, B., & Weil, M., with Calhoun, E. (2004). *Models of teaching* (7th ed.). Boston: Allyn & Bacon.

Kessler, R. (2000). *The soul of education: Helping students find connection, compassion, and character at school*. Alexandria, VA: ASCD.

Kirschner, P. A., Sweller, J., & Clark, R. E. (2006). Why minimal guidance during instruction does not work: An analysis of the failure of constructivist, discovery, problem-based, experiential, and inquiry-based teaching. *Educational Psychologist, 41*, 75–86.

Krajcik, J. S., & Blumenfeld, P. (2006). Project-based learning. In R. K. Sawyer (Ed.), *The Cambridge handbook of the learning sciences*. New York: Cambridge University Press.

Ladson-Billings, G. (2006). Yes, but how do we do it? Practicing culturally relevant pedagogy. In J. Landsman & C. W. Lewis (Eds.), *White teachers/diverse classrooms: A guide to building inclusive schools, promoting high expectations, and eliminating racism*. Sterling, VA: Stylus Publishing.

Lazarus, R. (1991). *Emotion and adaptation*. New York: Oxford University Press.

Leamnson, R. (1999). *Think about teaching and learning: Developing habits of learning with first year college and university students*. Sterling, VA: Stylus Publishing.

Lindley, J. (2010). Teachers' letters to Obama: The sleeping giant stirs. *Education Week, 29*(18), 23.

Lobel, A. (1980). *Fables*. New York: Harper & Row.

Marx, R. W., Blumenfeld, P. C., Krajcik, J. S., Fishman, B., Soloway, E., Geier, R., & Revital, T. T. (2004). Inquiry-based science in the middle grades: Assessment of learning in urban system reform. *Journal of Research in Science Teaching, 41*(10), 1063–1080.

Marzano, R. J., & Haystead, M. (2008). *Making standards useful in the classroom*. Alexandria, VA: ASCD.

Marzano, R., Pickering, D., & Pollock, J. (2001). *Classroom instruction that works: Research-based strategies for increasing student achievement*. Alexandria, VA: ASCD.

Mayer, R. E. (2004). Should there be a three-strikes rule against pure discovery learning? The case for guided methods of instruction. *American Psychologist, 59*, 14–19.

McCombs, B. & Miller, L. (2006). *Learner-centered classroom practices and assessments: Maximizing student motivation, learning, and achievement*. Thousand Oaks, CA: Corwin.

McTighe, J., Seif, E., & Wiggins, G. (2004). You can teach for meaning. *Educational Leadership, 62*(1), 26–30.

Meier, D. (2009). Democracy at risk: School's most pressing job is to teach the democratic life. *Educational Leadership, 66*(8), 45–48.

Miller, B. (2010). Math comes to YouTube at Palmyra Area Middle School. Retrieved February 2010 from http://www.pennlive.ocm/midstate/index.ssf/2010/02/

Miller, R. (1997). *What are schools for? Holistic education in American culture*. Brandon, VT: Holistic Education.

Murphy, M. M. (2006). *The history and philosophy of education: Voices of educational pioneers*. Upper Saddle River, NJ: Merrill/Pearson Education.

Noddings, N. (2005). What does it mean to educate the whole child? *Educational Leadership. 63*(1), 8–13.

Orlich, D. C., Harder, R. J., Callahan, R. C., Trevisan, M. S., & Brown, A. H. (2007). *Teaching strategies: A guide to better instruction* (8th ed.). Boston: Houghton Mifflin.

Ormrod, J. (2004). *Human learning* (4th ed.). Columbus, OH: Merrill/Pearson Education.

Palmer, P. (1998). *The courage to teach: Exploring the inner landscape of a teacher's life*. San Francisco: Jossey-Bass.

Payne, R. (2008). Nine powerful practices: Nine strategies help raise the achievement of students living in poverty. *Educational Leadership, 65*(7), 48–52.

Perkins-Gough, D. (2008). A focus on the whole child: Looking back, looking forward. *Educational Leadership, 65*(7), 96.

Piaget, J. (1926). *Judgment and reason in the child*. New York: Harcourt.

Piaget, J. (1969). *Psychologie et pedogogie*. Paris: Denoel/Garnier.

Postman, N. (1999). *Building a bridge to the 18th century: How the past can improve our future*. New York: Vintage Books.

Postman, N., & Weingartner, C. (1969). *Teaching as a subversive activity*. New York: Dell.

Price, V. C. (2006). I don't understand why my African American students are not achieving: An exploration of the connection among personal power, teachers' perceptions, and the academic engagement of African American students. In J. Landsman & C. W. Lewis (Eds.), *White teachers/diverse classrooms: A guide to building inclusive schools, promoting high expectations, and eliminating racism*. Sterling, VA: Stylus Publishing.

Pulliam, J., & Van Patten, J. (2007). *History of education in America* (9th ed.). Upper Saddle River, NJ: Merrill/Pearson Education.

Quintana, C., Shin, N., Norris, C., & Soloway, E. (2006). Learner-centered design. In R. K. Sawyer (Ed.), *The Cambridge handbook of the learning sciences* (pp. 119–134). New York: Cambridge University Press.

Ravitch, D. (2000). *Left back: A century of failed school reforms.* New York: Simon & Schuster.

Reisberg, D. (1997). *Cognition: Exploring the science of the mind.* New York: Norton.

Rendon, L. I. (2009). *Sentipensante pedagogy: Educating for wholeness, social justice and liberation.* Sterling, VA: Stylus Publishing.

Rivet, A., & Krajcik, J. (2004). Achieving standards in urban systemic reform: An example of a sixth grade project-based science curriculum. *Journal of Research in Science Teaching, 41*(7), 669–692.

Rogers, C. (1969). *Freedom to learn: A view of what education might become.* Columbus, OH: Merrill.

Rooney, J. (2009). This school is about kids. *Educational Leadership, 66*(8), 87–88.

Rosenzweig, M., & Bennett, E. (1978). Experiential influences on brain anatomy and brain chemistry in rodents. In G. Gottlieb (Ed.), *Studies on the development of behavior and the nervous system: Vol. 4. Early influences* (pp. 289–330). New York: Academic Press.

Rothstein, R., Wilder, T., & Jacobsen, R. (2007). Balance in the balance. *Educational Leadership, 64*(8), 9–14.

Sawyer, R. K. (2006). *The Cambridge handbook of learning sciences.* New York: Cambridge University Press.

Scardamalia, M., & Bereiter, C. (2006). Knowledge building: Theory, pedagogy, and technology. In R. K. Sawyer (Ed.), *The Cambridge handbook of learning sciences* (pp. 97–115). New York: Cambridge University Press.

Scherer, M. (2005). Valuing children. *Educational Leadership, 63*(1), 7.

Scherer, M. (2007). Why focus on the whole child? *Educational Leadership, 64*(8), 7.

Schmidt, W. (2004). A vision for mathematics. *Educational Leadership, 61*(5), 6–11.

Schmidt, W., Houang, R., & Cogan, L. (2002). A coherent curriculum: The case for mathematics. *American Educator, 26*(2), 10–26, 47–48.

Schmoker, M. (2009). Measuring what matters. *Educational Leadership, 66*(4), 70–74.

Schunk, D. H. (2008). *Learning theories: An educational perspective* (5th ed.). Columbus, OH: Merrill/Pearson Education.

Schwartz, M., Sadler, P. M., Sonnert, G., & Tai, R. (2008). Depth versus breadth: How content coverage in high school science courses relates to later success in college science coursework. *Science Education.*

Shayer, M., & Adey, P. (2002). *Towards a science of science teaching: Cognitive development and curriculum demand.* London: Heinemann Educational.

Shulman, L. (1999). Taking learning seriously. In D. DeZure (Ed.). (2000). *Learning from change: Landmarks in teaching and learning in higher education from Change Magazine, 1969–1999* (pp. 39–41). Sterling, VA: AAHE and Stylus Publishing.

Siegler, R. S. (1998). *Children's thinking* (3rd ed.). Upper Saddle River, NJ: Prentice Hall.

Simon, H. (1980). Problem solving and education. In D. Tuma & R. Reif (Eds.), *Problem solving and education: Issues in teaching and research* (pp. 81–96). Hillsdale, NJ: Erlbaum.

Simpson, T. L. (2002). Dare I oppose constructivist theory? *The Educational Forum, 66,* 347–354.

Sinatra, G. M., & Pintrich, P. R. (2003). *Intentional conceptual change.* Mahwah, NJ: Erlbaum.

Singley, K., & Anderson, J. (1989). *The transfer of cognitive skill.* Cambridge, MA: Harvard University Press.

Sire, J. W. (2004). *The universe next door* (4th ed.). Downers Grove, IL: Intervarsity Press.

Smith, F. (1988). *Joining the literacy club.* Portsmouth, NH: Heinemann.

Stemler, S., Grigorenko, E., Jarvin, L., & Sternberg, R. (2006). Using the theory of successful intelligence as a basis for augmenting AP exams in psychology and statistics. *Contemporary Educational Psychology, 31,* 344–376.

Sternberg, R. J. (2008). Assessing what matters. *Educational Leadership, 65*(4), 20–26.

Stiggins, R. (2007). Assessment through the students' eyes. *Educational Leadership, 64*(8), 22–26.

Stipek, D. (1993). *Motivation to learn: From theory to practice* (2nd ed.). Boston: Allyn & Bacon.

Sullo, B. (2007). *Activating the desire to learn.* Alexandria, VA: ASCD.

Sweller, J., & Levine, M. (1982). Effects of goal specificity on means-end analysis and learning. *Journal of Experimental Psychology: Learning, Memory, and Cognition, 8,* 463–474.

Thornton, H. (2006). Dispositions in action: Do dispositions make a difference in practice? *Teacher Education Quarterly, 33*(2), 53–68. San Francisco, CA: Caddo Gap Press. Retrieved January 2010 from http://eric.ed.gov/ERICWebPortal/custom/portlets/recordDetails/detailmini.jsp?_nfpb=tru

Toffler, A. (1970). *Future shock.* New York: Random House.

Treffinger, D. J., & Isaksen, S. G. (2005). Creative problem solving: The history, development, and implications for gifted education and talent development. *Gifted Child Quarterly, 49,* 342–353.

Trueblood, D. E. (1996). *A life of search.* Richmond, IN: Friends United Press.

Tsui, A. B. M. (2009). Distinctive qualities of expert teachers. *Teachers and Teaching: Theory and Practice, 15*(4), 421–439. Philadelphia: Routledge. Retrieved January 2010 from http://eric.ed.gov/ERICWebPortal/custom/portlets/record Details/detailmini.jsp?_nfpb=tru

Tuovinen, J. E., & Sweller, J. (1999). A comparison of cognitive load associated with discovery learning and worked examples. *Journal of Educational Psychology, 91,* 334–341.

Voss, J. (1987). Learning and transfer in subject-matter learning: A problem solving model. *International Journal of Educational Research, 11,* 607–622.

Vygotsky, L. S. (1978). *Mind in society.* Cambridge, MA: Harvard University Press.

Walsh, B. (2010). The electrifying Edison. *Time, 176*(1), 40–43.

Weigel, G. (1999). *Witness to hope: The biography of Pope John Paul II.* NY: HarperCollins.

Weiner, B. (2000). Intrapersonal and interpersonal theories of motivation from an attributional perspective. *Educational Psychology Review, 12,* 1–14.

Weissbourd, R. (2009). The schools we mean to be. *Educational Leadership, 66*(8), 27–31.

Welton, D. A., & Mallan, J. T. (1998). *Children and their world: Strategies for teaching social studies* (3rd ed.). Princeton, NJ: Houghton Mifflin.

Wikipedia (2008). Information age. Retrieved April 2008 from http://en.wikipedia.org/wiki/Information Age.

Willard, D. (1998). *The divine conspiracy: Rediscovering our hidden life in God.* San Francisco: HarperCollins.

Wingo, L. C. (2009). Student ability to excel lost. Retrieved September 2009 from http://www.bangordailynews.com/detail/120013.html

Wolk, S. (2008). Joyful learning can flourish in school—if you give joy a chance. *Educational Leadership, 66*(1), 8–15.

Wormelli, R. (2006). Busting myths about differentiated instruction. Retrieved July 2010 from http://docs.google.com/viewer?a=V&Q=cache:cqVIFAmECL8J:www.rivervalley,K12.oh.us.

Yarrow, A. L. (2009). State of mind. Retrieved October 2009 from http://www.edweek.org/ew/articles/2009/10/21/08publicagenda-ep.h29.html

Zakaria, F. (2006). We all have a lot to learn. *Newsweek, 147*(2), 37.

Zevin, J. (1969). Mystery island: A lesson in inquiry. *Today's Education, 58*(5), 42–43.

INDEX

Note: The letter f following a page number denotes a figure.

ABOUT THE AUTHORS

 **Tom Rosebrough** is executive dean of the College of Education and Human Studies at Union University and professor of education in Jackson, Tennessee. He has taught at all levels, from elementary school through college, from undergraduate through doctoral education. Rosebrough has taught public school, state university students, and private university students. He has published articles in state journals in educational leadership, national journals including *The Teaching Professor*, articles in two Canadian web journals, a book chapter, and frequent columns in various newsletters and newspapers. Rosebrough has been honored for his university teaching and scholarship; and, under his leadership, Union's School of Education has been nationally recognized for its learning community of ethical and moral dimensions. Rosebrough's interests include pedagogy, educational philosophy and ethics, and the history of education. He writes, does research, and presents at the local, state, national, and international levels and enjoys teaching on

Union's Jackson, Germantown, and Hendersonville campuses. He can be reached by e-mail at trosebro@uu.edu.

Ralph Leverett serves as program director for the Master of Education program at Union University and university professor of special education in Jackson, Tennessee. He has taught public school, state university, and private university students. Leverett has served as a public school teacher in several areas of special education, primarily students with low-incidence impairments and learning disabilities. He conducted a part-time private practice in speech-language pathology for 15 years; nearly half of that time was as a practitioner and consultant with the Missouri Department of Mental Health. Recently, Leverett served as a part-time speech-language pathologist for the West Tennessee School for the Deaf. His research interests and professional writings, which include journal articles and chapters in professional reference texts, relate to the language needs of special education students in inclusive settings. Leverett has presented workshops in these areas at the local, state, national, and international levels. In 2007, Leverett won the Jefferson Award given by Gannett Publishers for community service in the area of Education and Literacy in the Jackson-Madison County area. He can be reached by e-mail at rleveret@uu.edu.

Related ASCD Resources: Transformational Teaching

At the time of publication, the following ASCD resources were available; for the most up-to-date information about ASCD resources, go to www.ascd.org. ASCD stock numbers are noted in parentheses. You can search the complete archives of *Educational Leadership* at http://www.ascd.org/el.

Books

Activating the Desire to Learn, by Bob Sullo (#107009)

The Big Picture: Education Is Everyone's Business, by Dennis Littky and Samantha Grabelle (#104438)

The Classroom of Choice: Giving Students What They Need and Getting What You Want, by Jonathan C. Erwin (#104020)

Keeping the Whole Child Healthy and Safe: Reflections on Best Practices in Learning, Teaching, and Leadership, by Marge Scherer and the Educational Leadership Staff (#110130)

Learning for Keeps: Teaching the Strategies Essential for Creating Independent Learners, by Rhoda Koenig (#111003)

Multimedia

Emotional Intelligence Professional Inquiry Kit, by Pam Robbins and Jane Scott (#997146)

Creating a Healthy School Using the Healthy School Report Card, 2nd ed., by David K. Lohrmann (#110140)

Video

Educating Everybody's Children, Tape 4: Increasing Interest, Motivation, and Engagement (#400225)

THE WHOLE CHILD The Whole Child Initiative helps schools and communities create learning environments that allow students to be healthy, safe, engaged, supported, and challenged. To learn more about other books and resources that relate to the whole child, visit www.wholechildeducation.org.

For more information: send e-mail to member@ascd.org; call 1-800-933-2723 or 703-578-9600, press 2; send a fax to 703-575-5400; or write to Information Services, ASCD, 1703 N. Beauregard St., Alexandria, VA 22311-1714 USA.